THE LAST INVASION OF IRELAND

The Last Invasion of Ireland

The Last Invasion of Ireland

By

Eamonn Henry

Contents © 2019 Eamonn Henry
All Rights Reserved
Self-Published.
ISBN: 9781695191655;

The Last Invasion of Ireland

To:

Aine Devany, Alma Seale, Lincy Joseph, Mayda Tamayo, Bindumol Viswambharan, Michelle Banez, Supriya Thomas, Linet Siriac, Shirley Dizon, Mae Caparida, Ramon Embile, Lilia Dural, Mary Kate McCarthy, Eamon Morris, Charlene Lambert, Karen Thornton, & Geraldine Byrne

In appreciation of their professional standards at Unit One of the Renal Therapies Centre at Beaumont Hospital, Dublin 9.

Acknowledgements

I have used material from Irish and British national newspaper archives and indirectly from the official correspondence of Lord Cornwallis and the French generals, Humbert and Sarrazin. Furthermore, I found the website, www.frenchempire.net was an excellent resource also.

I have also relied very much on three long-forgotten books: "The French Invasion of Ireland in 98" by Valerian Gribayedoff, a Russian-born illustrator and newspaper reporter. Another was and an eye-witness account of what happened in Killala during the French occupation of the town, written by the Protestant bishop of the see, Joseph Stock and "History of the Irish Rebellion, 1798," by W. H. Maxwell was another that provided me with source material.

Finally, my research work would have been much harder if I did not have my late father's works. ("Folktales from County Mayo" and "Historic Tales of Mayo," to hand.

Foreword

"The Last Invasion of Ireland…"

On August 22, 1798, three French warships with over 1,100 officers and men onboard arrived without warning in Killala Bay and what followed was a truly remarkable episode in Irish history.

Under the command of General Jean-Joseph Humbert, the French invaders had taken control of North Mayo and had captured the county town, Castlebar, a mere five days later.

In doing so, they routed an enemy force of over 6,000 experienced troops, giving rise to the expression, "The Races of Castlebar."

Then, with all of Mayo north of Hollymount cleared of loyalist forces, Humbert inexplicably delayed a week in Castlebar giving the English an opportunity to regroup and to block his passage into the midlands.

Even so, he managed to get as far as Ballinamuck before he was forced to surrender to an enemy force of almost 39,000 men.

This study is an account of a most remarkable event in Irish history based on contemporary newspaper reports, official state papers and the personal narratives of some of the principal individuals involved.

Contents

Timeline of the Invasion..3
1 The Invasion: An Overview.......................................10
2 The French Are on The Say.......................................16
3 The Capture of Ballina..30
4 The Battle of Castlebar...40
5 Fatal Delay in Castlebar..48
6 The Long March..56
7 The Massacre of Ballinamuck...................................63
8 The Second Battle of Castlebar................................70
9 The French Officers in Killala..................................74
10 Anarchy in Killala..78
11 The End of the Rebellion...83
Appendices..93
12 Humbert's Subsequent Career...............................94
13 Jean Sarrazin...99
14 The Protestant Wind..103
15 Theobald Wolfe Tone..111
16 The Trial and Conviction of Mr. Bart. Teeling....127
17 Contemporary Newspaper Quotes.......................137

Timeline of the Invasion

AUGUST 6: General Humbert's self-styled "Army of Ireland", sailed from La Rochelle in three frigates. He had almost 1,100 soldiers under his command and a large supply of armaments and uniforms for the United Irishmen he anticipated would be waiting to greet him when he landed.

AUGUST 22: French forces landed at Kilcummin Strand on the western shore of Killala Bay, and captured Killala. Irish insurgents rushed to join them.

AUGUST 23-24: The Franco-Irish Army advanced on Ballina and captured it after a sharp skirmish.

AUGUST 25-26: Cornwallis, the Lord Lieutenant, sent an urgent request for reinforcements to England. Generals Lake, Hutchinson and Trench reinforced Castlebar, the major garrison town of north Connacht, against an anticipated attack.

AUGUST 26-27: Humbert left 200 men to protect Killala and keep his line of communications open when expected reinforcements should arrive. He took 1,500 French and Irish men with him and marched southwards from Ballina. It seemed that he was marching to the bridge on the Moy at Foxford. Several miles along the road he veered left and took his troops on a forced march down the western side of Lough Conn and descended on Castlebar from the northwest early on the morning of the 27th.

AUGUST 27: The English were anticipating an attack from the direction of Foxford and were completely surprised and outmanoeuvred. By mid-day the town was taken, and a huge supply of heavy guns and supplies was captured.

After some heavy fighting, the English panicked and fled south to Hollymount and Tuam and even as far as Athlone. This was probably one of the most embarrassing defeats in British military history. To the gleeful Irish, the rout became known as the "Races of Castlebar." Humbert sent a report to France asking for immediate reinforcements.

AUGUST 28: The English garrison evacuated Foxford and retreated to Boyle. Insurgents seized Westport, Newport, Ballinrobe, Swinford and Hollymount. Claremorris had already been taken. Cornwallis arrived in Athlone but decided not to counterattack until he had assembled a massive army.

AUGUST 31: Humbert, having consolidated his position, proclaimed a Republic of Connacht, and set up a civil administration and commenced training his Irish recruits. Many of those had defected from local militia units. He was a strict disciplinarian apparently and had several troublemakers shot.

SEPTEMBER 3-4: The English were by then ready to mount an attack on Castlebar. Humbert had anticipated this and evacuated Castlebar under cover of darkness, taking his army, now 3,000 strong, towards Sligo on a forced march. They covered 58 miles in 36 hours before camping at Bellaghy.

The long march had begun. Some Irish troops under French officers remained to protect Killala and receive the expected reinforcements.

SEPTEMBER 5: An English army from Sligo under Col. Vereker confronted the Franco-Irish army at Collooney. Humbert again outmanoeuvred them. Bartholomew Teeling, Humbert's aide-de-camp, showed outstanding bravery and the English retreated with heavy losses as far as Ballyshannon, County Donegal.

Cornwallis had now divided his army in two, one half under General Lake to pursue the enemy and the other half, under his own personal command, to protect the line of the River Shannon. The French and Irish were to be prevented from crossing the river and linking up with rebels in the midlands.

Meanwhile, the United Irishmen of Longford and Westmeath had assembled. They captured Wilson's Hospital near Mullingar but failed to take the town of Granard.

Humbert, on hearing of the midlands rising, decided to link up with the insurgents there. He was then near Manorhamilton but changed and went straight for Granard. He abandoned some of the heavier guns to make more speed. So far, he had eluded the cordon closing in around him. With some luck he hoped to slip past the net, reach Granard and then strike for Dublin which was virtually unprotected by then as most of the garrison have been moved to Connacht.

SEPTEMBER 6: The Franco-Irish army reached Drumkeerin in the evening. An envoy from General Lake offered terms for surrender but they were rejected.

SEPTEMBER 7: Before noon Humbert's army crossed the Shannon at Ballintra Bridge just south of Loch Allen, but they failed in an attempt to demolish the bridge behind them. His army showed signs of fatigue and skirmishes with the English advance guard became more frequent. The race for Granard quickened.

The Franco-Irish army reached Cloone, in South Leitrim, while Cornwallis, with 15,000 men was at Mohill, five miles away. Humbert got news that he was surrounded and outnumbered but decided to push on even if the best he could do was to make a token resistance before surrender.

SEPTEMBER 8: Cornwallis had got ahead and blocked the road to Granard at Ballinalee, while General Lake's army attacked from the rear. This was the Battle of Ballinamuck, County Longford.

The French surrendered after a fight of half an hour and were treated as prisoners of war. Five hundred Irish were massacred, while possibly up to 500 escaped. More were hanged at Longford, Ballinalee, and Carrick-on-Shannon.

SEPTEMBER 21-23: General Trench headed a three-pronged attack on Killala. On Sunday, the 23rd, the last stand was made by the insurgents, and 300 of them died, most of them being indiscriminately sabred by the dragoons at the spot still known as "casán an áir". (The path of slaughter)

The Last Invasion of Ireland

(A magnificent pyramid-like monument at French Hill, three miles south of Castlebar, marks the spot where a party of French cavalry, travelling under a flag of truce, were treacherously murdered by English forces. It was erected in 1876 and could be said to commemorate all of the 200 or so French soldiers who were killed, mostly at Castlebar and Collooney. The inscription reads: "In grateful remembrance of the gallant French soldiers who died fighting for the freedom of Ireland on the 27th August 1798. They shall be remembered forever.")

History as It Happened

"The Year of the French"

"The Year of the French" lasted just a month and a day but it was sadly remembered by Mayo people for generations afterwards for a host of wrong reasons.

The route, 225 km in length passes through four counties, Mayo, Sligo. Leitrim and Longford.

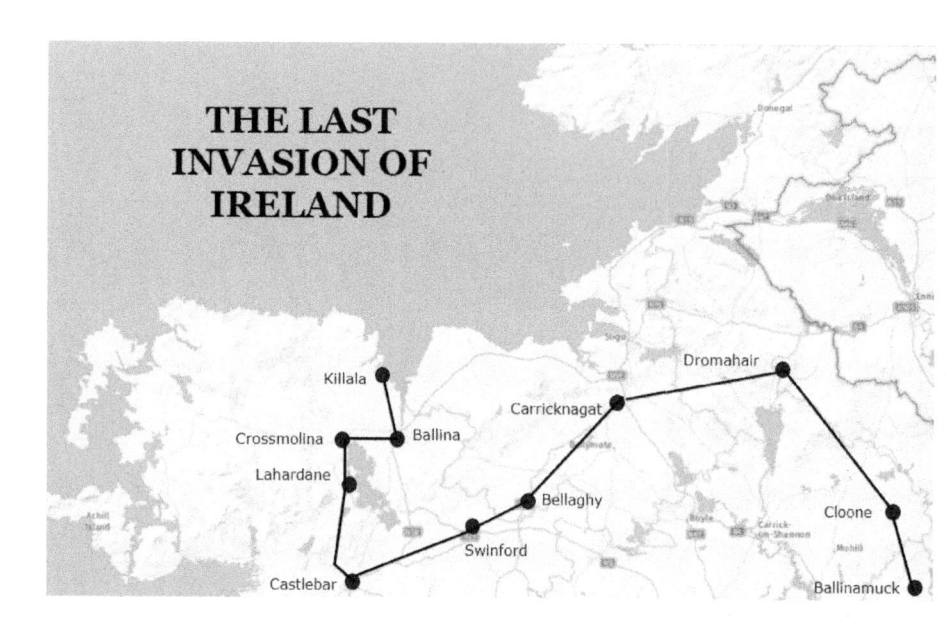

THE LAST INVASION OF IRELAND

The French arrived on 22 August and five days later, along with their new Irish allies they outed a much superior enemy force at Castlebar, and Humbert set up a Republic of Connaught and a form of civil administration before evacuating the town in the face of advancing English forces.

From there on, they met increasing resistance all the way until finally being forced to stop and give battle at Ballinamuck in North Longford on September 7.

1 The Invasion: An Overview

As the eighteenth century ended, England and France were at war.

Nothing out of the ordinary about this as both nations were extremely belligerent and there were never more than short periods of uneasy peace on both sides of the English Channel for centuries past.

Indeed, one could go further and say that since people first settled in both regions the ability to peacefully coexist seemed to be singularly lacking on both sides.

From an Irish perspective, these struggles usually meant next to nothing, because, for the common people, the struggle to survive was their priority concern.

However, this particular period in history saw Ireland being drawn into the conflict and in County Mayo one year above all others, stands out in folk memory ever since.

That was 1798, the "Year of the French."

One individual in particular changed the course of Mayo's history during that tumultuous period; a former dealer in rabbit skins named Jean-Joseph Amable Humbert.

He had been a colourful character by any standard long before he came to Ireland in 1798 and landed

The Last Invasion of Ireland

at Kilcummin Strand on the western shore of Killala Bay. He didn't come on his own but arrived at the head of a small French expeditionary force with the intention of joining up with the United Irishmen, who he believed were active in the midlands.

He intended, with their help, to drive the English out of the country and establish a republic, where all men would have had equal rights regardless of religion, race or political beliefs, as had happened in his native country.

This although he brought less than 1,100 men with him and had landed in the wrong place. Unfortunately for Humbert's plans, as it turned out. it was the wrong time also and the Irishmen who joined him were of the wrong type as well.

Still, his personal bravery and his undoubted tactical skills as well as the fearsome fighting qualities of his soldiers earned him the respect of friends and enemies alike.

To use a modern expression, they punched well above their weight.

> *Humbert's was a bold but wild experiment, but still it evinced the daring character of the adventurer. He had encountered difficulties that would have disheartened a soldier less enthusiastic. To land with 1,200 men, in a country in full military occupation – as Ireland then was – without money, necessities or any resources but what chance and talent gave, proved, indeed, that the French general was no common soldier.*
>
> W. H. Maxwell, "A History of the Irish Rebellion in 1798."

Their stay in Ireland lasted from August 22 to September 23, a month and a day and when the inevitable happened and the French surrendered to overwhelming enemy forces, they were treated as prisoners of war and safely repatriated to France.

But the native Irish who had sided with them were shown no mercy. They were treated as traitors - guilty of the crime of high treason. They had little choice but to fight on to the bitter end as surrendering would have meant certain death anyway.

Contemporary reports put the number who were killed in this last, desperate stand at Ballinamuck in County Longford at 400, with another 400 captured, most of whom were summarily executed, and an unknown number who managed to escape from the battlefield. Figures for this count were never verified but local tradition puts the figure at another 400 at the very least.

But for those rebels who remained behind in Mayo, the worst had still to come.

Now, the victorious English turned their attention to those Humbert had left behind when he set off on his ill-fated journey to Ballinamuck. Those were stationed in Ballina and Killala as Castlebar had been retaken by the enemy soon after Humbert's departure.

Like their comrades at Ballinamuck, those insurgents knew their fate and they also fought to the death. They defended every inch of ground from Foxford back to the streets of Killala, but the end result was always going to be inevitable.

Killala was finally overrun by English troops under General Trench on September 23, just over a month since the French arrived at Kilcummin strand.

For some time prior to Humbert's arrival, the English authorities were aware of the dangers of a French invasion of Ireland. The spirit of revolution was in the air; people throughout Europe were getting restless and were demanding change to the established order. France led the way in this regard.

Many French soldiers had fought on the side of the colonists during the American Revolution. "My enemies' enemy is my friend," could well have been their motto as they sided with those who wanted the right to independence, freedom of action and of thought.

Many of them, on their return home, brought this desire for change with them.

This in turn led to a growing sense of disenchantment with the autocratic policies of the nobility, with the king, Louis XVI, at their head. This growing sense of injustice was especially strong among the poorer classes of the city dwellers in Paris and in 1789, a large crowd attacked the Bastille, the state prison, and liberated the prisoners held there.

The French Revolution had begun.

By the time it ended every semblance of caste and noble privilege had been swept away, the king and queen and hundreds of the nobility had been executed and a Republic had been proclaimed. The rulers of the new state, the Directory, offered help to the poor and the outcast everywhere to help them get rid of their despotic regimes and to become masters of their own destiny.

Naturally enough, the monarchies throughout Europe were alarmed by this and they united forces to seek to destroy this republic before its influence threatened the very existence of every kingdom in Europe.

However, those who anticipated a speedy end to the French threat were in for a shock. The French army turned out to be a formidable fighting force and won battle after battle against the forces united against them. There were a number of reasons for this unexpected supremacy but the fact that the new state had a number of brilliant army commanders and one named Napoleon Buonaparte (or Bonaparte) was probably the most important of them all.

In 1795 at the age of 26 he had defeated the combined forces of the Italian and Austrian monarchies, along with the Hapsburg dynasty in modern day Germany and had conquered the Italian peninsula in less than a year. Naturally enough, he became a war hero in France and, as his popularity grew, the authority of the Directory waned.

Another man who joined the French army and was to rapidly through the ranks was Jean-Joseph Amable Humbert, a former dealer in furs and rabbit skins.

In 1794 at the age of 27, he had become a brigadier general.

Meanwhile in Ireland, news of the French exploits had begun to filter through and people, mainly liberal Presbyterians in the northeast, began to harbour ideas of a republic where all men, regardless of religion, race or colour would be united as Irishmen. This led to the formation of the United Irishmen.
The process wasn't straightforward, and this secret society didn't evolve overnight but by the mid-nineties, groups of like-minded individuals were coming together to form debating

societies and discussion forums where the ideals promoted by the French revolutionaries were discussed.

A Dublin-born barrister named Theobald Wolfe Tone was one of the most prominent members and he went to Paris in 1795 to petition the Directory to send assistance to the United Irishmen.

Meanwhile the people of rural Ireland and of Mayo in particular were almost completely unaware of the momentous events unfolding on the continent or that the doctrine of "liberté, egalité, fraternité" was changing the outlook of many liberal minded people in the northeast of the country and in Dublin also.

To all intents and purposes, the land west of the Shannon was a cultural and economic backwater and life was a matter of unrelenting hardship for the vast majority of people, invariably Catholic and tenants of landlords who differed from them in every conceivable way and who were determined to deny them any form of freedom or expression.

When they were given an opportunity to strike back at their oppressors, they were hell bent on revenge and cared little for "liberté, egalité, fraternité" for all.

2 The French Are on The Say

On the evening of August 22 of that year, three French naval ships suddenly appeared in Killala Bay and anchored off Kilcummin Head on the western shore of the bay.

It turned out that there were 1,060 French soldiers onboard under the command of General Jean-Joseph Humbert. The ships were flying English flags and onlookers thought they were a detachment sent by the Royal Navy to patrol the North Mayo No one really knows why Humbert decided to land at such an isolated spot on the rocky North Mayo coast.

It may have been that adverse weather conditions forced him ashore at this place or fear of encountering a Royal Navy patrol further on if he attempted to land in Donegal, where he had heard that United Irishmen were active. But Henry O'Kane, one of his trusted aides, was a native of this area and was with him on this expedition so the place may have been chosen in advance.

The reaction locally was entirely predictable. The Loyalists were elated because British warships in the bay meant security for all; all, that is of their community. Most of the poorer people, all Catholics, had their hopes of freedom from oppression dashed once again. For them, there would be no new and joyous tomorrow but a continuation of their miserable lot.

For some years now, local people had been getting third- or fourth-hand accounts of the war raging on the continent and every local, Catholic or Protestant, would have heard of Napoleon Bonaparte and his "la grande armeé," the formidable blue coat soldiers who had struck fear into everybody who opposed them. For some weeks past, rumours were rife that a French invasion fleet had sailed from La Rochelle and was bound for Ireland, but nobody knew where or when they would land or what size this army would be.

All along the western seaboard nerves were on edge and tensions between the communities were heightened. The poor may not have had their human rights, but they did have their stories and songs to commemorate past glories or to pine for new tomorrows.

One of the songs that was popular with the peasantry and others of the lower classes was the "Shan Van Vocht." The name is a phonetic version of the Gaelic term, "An tSean Bhean Bhocht," meaning the poor old woman, a figurative name for Ireland.

The Catholic poor may have had songs like this one but the Protestant rich had power and intended holding on to it by all means possible.

The Shan Van Vocht
"Oh! the French are on the say," says the
Sean van Vocht,
"Oh! the French are on the say," says the
Sean van Vocht,

"The French are in the Bay, they'll be here at break of day,
And the Orange will decay," says the Sean van Vocht,
"And the Orange will decay," says the Sean van Vocht.

"And where will they have their camp?" says the Sean van Vocht,
"And where will they have their camp?" says the Sean van Vocht.
"On the Curragh of Kildare and the boys will all be there
With their pikes in good repair." says the Sean van Vocht,
"With their pikes in good repair." says the Sean van Vocht.
"And what will the yeomen do?" says the Sean van Vocht,
"And what will the yeomen do?" says the Sean van Vocht,
"What will the yeomen do but throw off the red and blue,
And swear they will be true to the Sean van Vocht?
And swear they will be true to the Sean van Vocht?"

> *"Then what colour will be seen?" says the Sean van Vocht,*
> *"Then what colour will be seen?" says the Sean van Vocht,*
> *"What colour should be seen where our fathers' homes have been*
> *But our own immortal green?" says the Sean van Vocht,*
> *"But our own immortal green?" says the Sean van Vocht.*

Suddenly, on the evening of August 22nd the people of Kilcummin and the surrounding area felt that, with three Royal Navy ships anchored off-shore, there would be no incursion in their area and for the present it was back to normality once again.

But after a short period of time, onlookers on the shore began to realise that things were not what they had seemed to be. They saw a number of small boats plying from ships to shore and returning for more cargo. Included with the equipment and baggage were numbers of blue clad soldiers who were assembling in formation on the strand.

Word was brought to the people of Killala, several miles southeast of Kilcummin, that a large body of soldiers, armed and wearing blue uniforms were marching along the road to the town.

There could no longer be any doubt; the long- anticipated arrival of the French had become a reality and, what's more, they were going to attack the little town. According to the folklore of the area, upon Humbert's coming ashore, a local musician took out a penny whistle and produced a spirited jig. the French general (much to the delight of the gathering) danced a step or two.

Captain Kirkwood, commander of the local yeomen and the detachment of soldiers stationed in the area, prepared to resist the invaders and drew his men up in battle formation. Humbert sent his adjutant, Sarrazin, forward in advance of the main body of the attacking column to reconnoitre the defenses of the town.

He decided to deploy a squad of sharpshooters to pin Kirkwood's defenders down and marched his men straight into the town and up through the main street. This bold move had the desired effect.

The sight of soldiers in blue marching straight towards them caused the defenders to panic and run away without putting up any sort of organised resistance. They didn't know the size of the attacking force and felt that survival trumped over valour so they panicked and fled.

French soldiers in the continental wars then raging in Europe had earned a fearsome reputation and had been successful in every conflict to date. They caused panic wherever they went. Killala was to be no exception and neither were Ballina nor Castlebar when the French moved to attack their defences.

Kirkwood's troops had erected makeshift barricades to prevent the bluecoats taking over the main street but when the enemy suddenly appeared in view and, with bayonets fixed, decided to charge the defences, those behind the barricades lost their nerve and fled for safety to the nearby castle.

They attempted to block the entrance, but their efforts were in vain as Sarrazin's men forced the gate open and, after some spirited resistance, the defenders surrendered and lay down their weapons.

Now they and the loyalist inhabitants of the town felt in grave danger and had good reason to fear for their lives as discontented locals from throughout the region thronged into Killala, anxious to assist Humbert in every way they could.

He was lucky that he had a former priest, Henry O'Kane with him. O'Kane (or O'Keon) was a native of North Mayo and spoke French fluently so his services as an interpreter were very important.

Another trusted Irish man was Bartholomew Teeling, a native of Lurgan in County Down who was Humbert's aide-de-camp.

Most certainly, there would have been widespread slaughter if Humbert had not made it clear from the start that he would not condone such violence. He assured the Protestant Bishop, Francis Stock, whose palace he was taking over, that he had come to deliver the people of Ireland from tyranny and oppression and that the lives and property of the bishop and the other Loyalists were not going to be harmed.

It seems that he kept his word and maintained strict discipline throughout his time in Ireland. He had several of the most unruly recruits shot for insubordination and one young recruit got a severe caning because he discharged a musket accidentally and almost shot Humbert in the process.

The bishop was highly complimentary of Humbert and his troops.

An appreciation of his character was first published in an anonymous pamphlet in 1800. It is generally accepted that the author was Bishop Stock.

> "Humbert, the leader of this singular body of men, was himself as extraordinary a personage as any in his army. Of a good. height and shape, in the full vigor of life, prompt to decide, quick in execution, apparently master of his art, you could not refuse him the praise of a good officer, while his physiognomy forbade you to like him as a man. His eye, which was small and sleepy (the effect, probably, of much watching), cast a sidelong glance of insidiousness, and even of cruelty: it was the eye of a cat preparing to spring upon her prey. His education and manners were indicative of a person sprung from the lower order of society, though he knew how (as most of his countrymen can do) to assume, where it was convenient, the deportment of a gentleman. For learning he had scarcely enough to enable him to write his name. His passions were furious, and all his behavior seemed marked with the characters of roughness and violence. A narrower observation of him, however, served to discover that much of this roughness was the result of art, being assumed with the view of extorting

by terror a ready compliance with his commands."

On the following morning, the 23rd, the French commander issued a proclamation that had been carefully prepared by himself and the Irish officers accompanying the expedition.

It was couched in the flowery language of the day, and, translated into Irish, was well calculated to stir the emotions of the common people.

When the town had been secured and all English security forces had been cleared, Humbert called a meeting in the town centre to address the locals, both Protestant and Catholic.

First, a French soldier climbed to the roof of the Episcopal palace and lowered the British flag. Then a green flag, with a harp embroidered in the centre, and bearing the motto, "Erin go Bragh," rose slowly from its base, greeted by a triple salvo and the cheers of the large group of onlookers. The inhabitants of Killala had fully realised the significance of the situation, and the large majority being rebellious, the invading army was surrounded by enthusiastic supporters, eager to offer help and cooperate in any way they could.

Naturally enough, the Protestants in the town saw things in a very different light.

To what extent the leaders of the insurgents were prepared for Humbert's coming may be gathered from the (somewhat biased) statement of a loyalist inhabitant, who declared that a number of them appeared from the start in uniforms provided by their "new friends."

> *"Nothing could exceed the consternation which prevailed throughout the town, the loyalists every moment expecting to be butchered in cold blood. Men, women and children, drowned in tears, attempted to escape, but in vain. Every avenue leading from Killala was thronged by rebels making in to receive the fraternal embrace, whose eyes indicated. the malignity of their hearts, No one was permitted to depart but on business which concerned the invaders."*

The issuing of the proclamation had the desired effect and hundreds of local people rushed forward to offer their services to the triumphant French. The news of the French arrival was spread far and wide by messengers on horseback.

"Tá do chairde ag Cill Alaidh," was the message they carried. (Your friends are at Killala is the meaning of this slogan.)

However, it was clear that Humbert had mixed feelings about the worth of his new allies as his officers struggled to impose some semblance of order on the eager but thoroughly undisciplined newcomers.

It was painfully obvious and becoming clearer by the hour that those who rushed to aid him were not too interested in the rights of the common people or the brotherhood of all, regardless of religion, race or creed!

Revenge was on their minds; revenge for past wrongs as well as plunder for personal gain were the main considerations of those who threw in their lot with the French in Killala and every other place they passed through. He knew they lacked neither courage nor conviction, but he had his doubts from the outset that their lack of discipline and unwillingness to accept discipline might make them more of a hindrance than a help in the conflicts that they were going to face.

Here the preparations for an active campaign were being pushed with great energy. Humbert's programme being to organize a regular army composed of Irishmen, he assembled all the leading agitators of the vicinity, to obtain their aid and counsel. It was at this period, already, that he discovered the great gulf which separated the French Republican and Freethinker from the Irish patriot and Catholic.

Humbert, a soldier of the nation that had driven the pope from Italy, found himself, to his surprise, the would-be deliverer of a race to whom the pontiff was but one remove from the Deity itself. The situation was as startling as it was unexpected, not to him alone but to every one of his followers, sons of the great revolution, worshippers at the shrine of "Liberty" and "Reason," to whom the old religions, one and all, were part and parcel of a system for the enslaving of the human mind and body. From the neck of every one of the sturdy peasants who had by hundreds gathered. in front of the castle, clamouring for arms and the

opportunity to march against the common foe, hung a square piece of brown cloth with the letters I. H. S inscribed on it.
These were scapulars intended to arm them with fresh courage and protect them from danger in the hour of trial. Some carried banners decorated with the embroidered image of the Virgin Mary and the Infant Jesus; some held up crucifixes for their companions to adore. All greeted the French as defenders of the true religion and asked for the confiscation of all Protestant property; and the more bloodthirsty even demanded that the entire extirpation of the heretics be commenced without delay."

Gribayedoff

To put it mildly, this was not what Humbert had been expecting when he set sail on his mission to liberate the Irish people from tyranny and injustice. Was he going to exchange one form of savagery for another?

To him the situation was embarrassing in the extreme. On the one hand, by rejecting the demands of the insurgents he risked losing their much-needed assistance; on the other, by listening to them he would be violating the rules of war and exposing himself and his men to the vengeance of the enemy in case of defeat. The insurgents were therefore told in unmistakable terms that all attempts to harm any loyalist would be met with summary punishment of the offender.

> "A correspondent mentions that the conduct
> of the French soldiery, who landed
> at Killala, to the Rebels and Deserters who
> joined them was highly ludicrous and at the
> same time most wisely cautious.
> They affected to meet the Rebels with
> Republican Fraternity, saying "Erin
> go Braugh," but when the Erinites would make
> too free and want to mess with them, the French
> soldiers, not liking too close an acquaintance
> with traitors, always desired the Rebels in
> broken English to keep their own company."
>
> (Freeman's Journal Thursday, October 25, 1798)

The next task for his little army and the horde of new recruits was an attack on Ballina, seven miles south of Killala. Having taken control of Killala, the French spent the afternoon transporting munitions and military equipment from the ships to the town. Humbert informed Bishop Stock that he would have to requisition horses, cattle and general food stocks as the expedition had sailed from La Rochelle before all supplies had been loaded. However, he was careful to add that all goods required would be paid for and the owners would be given vouchers payable on the Irish Directory.

According to local tradition, Humbert got very drunk on all nights he spent in Mayo. He rode a white charger and went through the streets, waving his cockade at both French and Irishmen alike and greeting them all with a hearty "Erin go Bragh!"

This may have been a rumour, spread by his detractors, of which there were many, but it's possible that when he saw the magnitude of the task facing him, he decided to unwind in the only way possible under the circumstances!

After all, he had been led to believe from what Wolfe Tone and other United Irishmen had been telling the Directory that squadrons of well-drilled United Irishmen would be ready to join him as soon as he landed in Ireland. To put it mildly, those he now saw milling about him were not what he had been led to expect would be waiting to greet him.

The French were amazed and disgusted at the impoverished state of the Irish poor. Captain Jobit, one of the French officers wrote an account of what he saw and how he felt.

> *"We were astonished by the extreme poverty which appeared everywhere before our eyes. Never has any country presented such an unhappy perspective, the women and children are practically naked and have as their only shelter a small bad cottage which barely covers them from the ravages of the season. Moreover, they share this primitive habitation with everything from the farmyard. Their daily food is potatoes and sour milk, practically never bread."*

The thought surely crossed Humbert's mind at this time and at many others to come, that if only he had the pleasure of Monsieur Tone's presence there and then, he'd give him a good kick up the derrieré!

However, there was little time for speculation and, with Killala secured, Humbert now looked southwards to the next garrison town.

3 The Capture of Ballina

Ballina lies approximately 8 miles southwest of Killala. Sarrazin (provisionally promoted to Général de Brigade by Humbert the previous day) led a mixed force of some 500 French and Irish on the morning of August 24th and marched on Ballina. His primary objective was the capture of the town and then he intended to strike southwest for the county town of Castlebar in central Mayo.

He knew Cornwallis, the Lord Lieutenant, also realised the strategic importance of the county town and would be sending all available troops to that area. In those times there were few roads worthy of the name in the west of Ireland and as most of the better ones in Mayo connected with Castlebar, Humbert realised that if he had control of the town, he would have numerous options to consider.

But first Ballina had to be secured and while he had the advantage to be gained from the collapse of the enemy forces at Killala, he decided to press onwards, leaving the opposition with little or no time to reorganise.

With Sarrazin again leading the vanguard, the Franco-Irish force encountered the enemy's defenders about two miles north of the town. The commander of the Ballina garrison, Colonel Sir

Thomas Chapman, advanced up the Killala road with a force of several hundred soldiers and militia and took up a strong defensive position. Chapman's force confronted the French, about two miles outside the town, and a brisk fight ensued. The British were holding their own, until out of the darkness on their left, burst a howling mob of Irish rebels led by French Colonel Fontaine. At the same time, Sarrazin had ordered his men to fix bayonets and launch a frontal assault. The defenders broke and ran.

The people of Ballina were thrown into utter confusion when the disorganised remnants of Chapman's army arrived back, bloody and disorganised. All the townspeople took refuge in their homes, the Catholics in fear of the military and the Protestants in fear of the French. The Royal troops made no effort to prevent the French overrunning the town and kept fleeing southwards towards Foxford.

There is a street in Ballina today known as Bohernasop, the road of the torches in Gaelic. The inhabitants of the area lit little torches of hay or straw or whatever came to hand to guide the French as darkness fell. One old resident dragged his feather mattress outside and set it on fire.

Humbert now had approximately 800 Frenchmen and between 1,200 and 1,500 Irish rebels.

The remainder of the invading force, about 200, were left behind in Killala under the command of Lieutenant-Colonel Charost to guard the large supply of ammunition that had been brought from France with the invading army. He had another pressing reason to leave a strong body of men behind. He wanted to ensure the safety of the Protestant population as he knew they could be slaughtered by the more extreme Irish rebels who remained behind when the main body left the town to march on Ballina. He was also aware of the threat posed by a seaward invasion by the British based in Sligo with a view to cutting his lines of communication.

At the moment he was in the ascendant, but he knew a mistake in timing or in action could be disastrous. He knew he had to keep pressing ahead and take Castlebar before Cornwallis or his generals, Lake or Hutchinson, managed to reach there and deny him access to the roads to the east.

His Irish recruits and his soldiers had acquitted themselves very well in the skirmish against Chapman, but Humbert was, by now, very much disillusioned by the calibre of the peasantry who came forward and thrown in their lot with his. He and his officers tried with all their might to be as conciliatory as possible and stopped at nothing short of removing protection from the frightened Protestant population in order to appease them.

Another contemporary account was also critical of the relationship between the locals and the French invaders.

> *"The French army is said to have at their landing at Killala Bay amounted to 1,060 men, who by various accidents have been reduced to 800. The General, Humbert, has distributed amongst the Rebels, arms and cloathing for 3,000 men, but has never been able to collect more than 1,500 of them for service. In short, they find themselves baffled, disappointed and*

> *betrayed, insomuch that they have begun to quarrel among themselves; some veteran Grenadiers from the army of Italy have remonstrated very loudly with their General, as having inveigled them to utter destruction. Upon the whole, we are happy that the experiment has been made; those of the invading army who may chance to return home will, no doubt, most feelingly demonstrate to their Rulers the wild absurdity of hoping to succeed in an invasion of Ireland."*

Then Henry O'Kane, a priest and a member of Humbert's officer corps came to the rescue. He mounted a rostrum in the market place in Ballina and addressed the restless multitude.

Because the throng knew he was a priest and furthermore, was a native of North Mayo, they quietened down and stood silently to hear what he had to say. He told them the following story in Irish.

He dreamt, he said that the Mother of God appeared to him in a dream one night and told him the sad tale of Ireland's suffering. O'Kane told his audience that he had other worries at the time, and he put the apparition to one side but a few nights later, the heavenly visitor reappeared and told him even more melancholy news about the poor suffering people he had left behind when he came to France. She urged him once more to return home to aid his suffering, defenceless people.

Once again, he had more pressing issues at that time and, again, he failed to heed the pleas of the Mother of God. So, she made a third appearance and this time she gave him a good box on the ear! That, he assured his spellbound audience was enough to convince him that the Madonna was moved by the suffering of her poor Irish children and wanted him to intervene on her behalf. He had then approached the French Directory and persuaded them to undertake this expedition.

He assured his audience that the result of the present campaign had to be a foregone conclusion as the Mother of God had advised it and she would never turn her back on her children.

All present gave him a rousing cheer when he had finished his exhortation and not a single dissenting voice was to be heard!

He had bought time for the invaders, but time was a commodity in short supply as Humbert, O'Kane and their colleagues knew only too well. He entered Ballina early on the morning of the 24th, a Sunday, and having had a few hours rest, he and his entire corps got ready to proceed to Castlebar. Sympathisers had been bringing him a steady stream of information about the enemy's movements and it was clear that they also understood the strategic importance of Castlebar.

It was three o'clock in the afternoon by then and the outlook was for heavy rain. Nobody in the little cortege had any reason to feel happy. The French had landed at Kilcummin on the 22nd of the month, a bare three days before, and had been fighting or marching almost continually and this after spending three weeks at sea since they left La Rochelle.

Humbert's account of the weather they experienced makes clear that they had a very stormy crossing so obviously the troops were extremely fatigued. Now they were in a race against time as their general knew he would have to take, and secure Castlebar before the English had time to reinforce the town's defences.

The French now faced the prospect of having to force their way through the defences at Foxford bridge and then continue on their way through hostile countryside where they would have to contend with snipers and ambushes and their advance would be contested every step of the way. If he continued on as he appeared to be doing, Humbert would inevitably be facing heavy losses. But he didn't intend to follow the obvious route and waited until the last possible moment to change his tactics.

In his eyes, his new-found recruits to the campaign were a mixed blessing; they were not the well-drilled squadrons of United Irishmen he had expected to be there to greet him as one could imagine.

That they were courageous to a fault and ready to fight could not be denied but, almost to a man, they were incorrigible. The concept of military discipline was something they just did not possess, and Humbert was beginning to realise that they never would. He knew he desperately needed reinforcements and was willing to accept help from wherever it came from, but he had to spend time and effort keeping his Irish recruits under effective control.

The anger that they felt towards their Protestant oppressors was understandable, but he knew he would always have to keep strict discipline if he was to have any hope of succeeding in his mission.

The Irish for their part were beginning to get restless and many were already having second thoughts about their involvement in Humbert's plans. Some had already slipped away and gone back home, taking in some cases new uniforms and military equipment with them. Even at this early stage of the invasion, tensions were heightened between the common French soldiers and their rebel counterparts.

However, the Franco--Irish force hadn't run entirely out of luck. The officer in overall command of the British forces facing them was General Lake, who had distinguished himself by his cruelty towards the local population when suppressing the rising in Wexford during the summer of that year. Lake's inhumanity was matched by his arrogance and his belief that neither the French fighters or their locally recruited allies would be a match for his men. As it turned out, he seriously underestimated the threat from the invaders.

Also, tensions were mounting between units of the military then arriving in Castlebar from other parts of the country.

> *"…….Fights and broils between the regulars and the militia were of hourly occurrence, and even indulgence in intoxicating liquors seems to have been not infrequent. The disgraceful scenes reached their climax on Sunday night, the 26th, after the main body of the Longford militia had entered town. The men were bivouacked on the green, eating bread and cheese, when a shot, discharged from a window close by, fell in their midst. Immediately a stupendous uproar ensued. "In the dark of the night," wrote an eye- witness, "four thousand*

> *enraged soldiers in the town! A noise arose-the clamor of irritated passions. Arms clashed against each other, and glass flew from windows, whilst the enraged men called for vengeance on the culprit. The general shouted for the officer commanding (Captain Chambers) to stand in the street until the affair should be over. The fellow who fired the shot fled off when he thought he had kindled a flame which would destroy the town. I am told if there had not been instant peace the general would have caused the cannon to be brought to bear on the street and swept it with grapeshot; but glory to the Prince of Peace! he gave us a silent street in ten minutes.*
>
> Gribayedof

All credible accounts put the number of British troops, regular soldiers and militia, at upwards of 8,000 men, either based in Castlebar or assembled in Foxford to prevent the French from crossing the river. Humbert had at most 1,500, a mixture of tired French soldiers and of unruly natives, most of whom were proving to be extremely troublesome.

But he kept his reservations secret and, with banners waving and drums beating, his little force set off southwards towards Foxford

He knew he was certain to meet with strong opposition at the bridge over the River Moy and he also knew spies would be observing his preparations and reporting back to enemy forces in the area so he kept his true intentions hidden and made ready to march as anticipated.

His army set off in formation on the road south but several miles outside the town, he veered to the right and marched to Lahardane on the western shore of Lough Conn. Castlebar lies roughly 15 kilometres southwest of Lahardane and in Humbert's time there was no connecting road worthy of the name. However, there was a rough path, no more than a goat trail in places, and Humbert decided to take this. It was truly a desperate decision by a driven man; few would have contemplated it and the English waiting to defend the bridge at Foxford or who had gathered in Castlebar were blissfully unaware of what their adversary was going to do.

With a local scout to guide them, Humbert's little army pressed on through the darkness and the rain, slipping and sliding about in the mud. They had brought two curricle guns, light cannon on single axle carts, with them but after a few miles it became clear that the farm horses sequestered in Killala, were not able to pull them or the ammunition carts any further. Nothing daunted, volunteers from the Irish rebels came forward and carried the guns and supplies on their backs for the rest of the journey. The trail wound around the base of Nephin mountain, through rocky foothills alternating with boggy marshes for almost all of the way from Lahardane to the outskirts of Castlebar. Humbert's journey in pitch darkness and in driving rain would be remarkable by any standard but he and his men had already fought two pitched battles in less than 24 hours and had no opportunity to sleep for more than two days.

It was no wonder that their enemies were scared at the sight of blue coats on the field of battle!

4 The Battle of Castlebar

Dawn was breaking when they somehow managed to make it as far as the Windy Gap, a pass over the mountains northwest of Castlebar.

They still had several miles to go before they reached the town and they were halfway there before their presence was spotted. General Lake realised he had been wrongfooted and gave orders to sound the alarm and make ready for the attack. There was a good degree of confusion between the various units of English troops based in the town and it took the best part of an hour before they were ready to face their adversaries.

By sunrise, the attackers had advanced to the outskirts of the town and the defenders had managed to assume some sort of battle formation and were prepared to confront them.

The element of surprise had favoured Humbert, but the numerical odds were stacked heavily against him; he was outnumbered by at least four to one.

The English were drawn up in three lines on a hill to the northeast of the town, known as Mount Burren, and selected in anticipation of a French attack from the Foxford direction. It is understandable that in the general confusion and the unexpectedness of the direction the French were coming from, the defenders may indeed have outnumbered their attackers but were very much in a disorganised state.

Even so, given their overwhelming superiority of numbers and the fact that their opponents had been steadily marching for fifteen hours without food or rest through the bogs and mountains to the north of Castlebar, the English commanders must have been extremely confident that the result would be a foregone conclusion.

Looking across at the massed lines of red coats waiting to oppose him, Humbert must have felt the same way. But he was stubborn and steadfast in his beliefs and would never dream of dishonouring his nation's flag. Accordingly, he drew his men up in battle formation and prepared to charge the enemy.

He began by drawing up a squadron of the rebel recruits and directed them to overrun the English outposts and directly attack the artillery positioned behind them. The Irish promptly obliged and charged pell mell at the hated enemies with pikes and pitchforks and heedless of danger. Sarrazin with his experienced Grenadiers followed closely behind.

The advance enemy positions were easily taken, and the Irish charged directly at the gun units commanded by a Captain Shortall. He held fire until the attackers were nearly up to his position and then he trained his guns on the incomers and gave the order to fire at will

The attackers were cut to pieces with dead and dying everywhere. The instant carnage was too much for the simple peasants, most of whom had probably never heard a gunshot before. They scattered on all sides and rushed down the hillside in terror, most of them took no further part in the battle.

But their brave assault on the artillery position had achieved its main purpose as their heroics allowed Sarrazin and his men to come much closer to the defenders without suffering heavy casualties. The Irish has shielded their advance with great loss to themselves.

However, Sarrazin found the going difficult and was unable to rush his opponents' line for some considerable time and at equally considerable loss. It looked as if Humbert's brave manoeuvre was going to prove a failure. This seemed inevitable

after the French had rounded up some cattle and tried to use them as a shield by driving the beasts on before them as they tried once more to overwhelm the enemy positions but, like the Irish rebels a short time previously, the noise and slaughter terrorised the poor cattle and they also turned and fled.

The immediate effect of this was that the frightened beasts fled back the way they had come and nearly trampling the men they were designed to protect in the process.

But Humbert, overseeing all of this realised that the English were poorly led as they had failed to press home the advantage presented to them. He decided on a bold stroke. He spread is men out in a single line and directed them to attack the enemies entire front. The English reacted with amazement, followed by hesitation and doubt as they saw the thin line of blue coats marching resolutely toward them, bayonets at the ready.

Some of the more experienced defenders had already come face to face with Napoleon's "la grande armeé" before and their recollections were not happy ones. The infantry faltered first, and their fire was poorly aimed and uncoordinated while the cavalry behind them had to watch and wait as the foot soldiers

The Last Invasion of Ireland

milling about in front of them blocked their way. The intrepid French kept on coming, whereas the English front ranks grew more panic stricken as the blue coats came closer. Then a detachment of chasseurs under Colonel Ardouin suddenly attacked the left flank of the English army. That was the proverbial straw that broke the camel's back.

The massed ranks of infantry broke ranks and ran, leaving dead and dying comrades scattered behind them. The artillery unit was in trouble also and Captain Shortall was nearly captured in the ensuing rush to vacate their positions by the gunners under his command. He was dragged from his charger by a French officer and would have been shot but his boxing skills saved him. He engaged his opponent in hand to hand combat and succeeded in knocking him out before mounting his horse again and fleeing the battlefield.

The dramatic collapse of the infantry and the loss of Shortall's cannon alarmed General Lake and he ordered a full-scale retreat. The retreat had soon turned into a rout despite the best efforts of some of the officers to control their men. Even those who were left to guard St Mary's Church Protestant church fell victim to the hysteria sweeping through the ranks. Though they had stout walls to protect them, at the first sight of French uniforms, they turned and ran, scrambling over tombstones in their haste to escape,

But the battle was not over yet. Some remnants of the English army maintained enough composure to provide cover for their fleeing comrades. From behind hedges and fences they attempted to slow the French advance down with sustained musket fire and a group of Highlanders attempted to make a stand in the town square. To dislodge them Humbert sent Fontaine and Sarrazin with a company of infantry.

A Protestant clergyman who was an eyewitness to this phase of the battle described what was happening:

> *"A Protestant citizen present at the battle related some of the details of this conflict: "Colonel Miller," he said, "rushed into the town crying: 'Clear the street for action!! when in a moment, as a dam bursting its banks, a mixture of soldiers of all kinds rushed in at every avenue; a sergeant desired that every woman should go to the barracks; but Dr. Hennin's, another family and mine retired into a house, fell on our knees, and there remained in prayer until the town was taken. Four brave Highlanders at a cannon kept up a brisk fire on the French, but were killed while loading, the gunner taken, and the guns turned on our men. Now the street action became hot; 'before it was peal answering peal, but now thunder answering thunder; a black cloud of horrors hid the light of heaven, the messengers of death groping their way, as in gloomy hell, whilst the trembling echoes which shook our town concealed the more melancholy groans of the dying.*
> *When the French approached the new jail, our sentinel (a Fraser Fencible) killed one Frenchman, charged and killed another, shot a*

The Last Invasion of Ireland

> *third and a fourth, and, as he fired at and killed*
> *the fifth, a number rushed up the steps, dashed*
> *his brains out, tumbling him from his stand,*
> *and the sentry-box on his body."*

Gribayedoff

When the main portion of the town was in their hands, the French turned their attention to the bridge. There, a body of British with a curricle gun had taken stand. A desperate melee was the result. Worked up to a pitch of fury, neither side gave nor demanded quarter.

The defenders of the bridge consisted of the remnants of many of the regiments present on the field an hour before. There were some Longford and Kilkenny men, a sprinkling of "Frasers," and a corporal's guard or so of the 6th Regiment. The gun itself was worked by the few remaining survivors of Captain Shortall's Royal Irish Artillery Corps. The French began by installing themselves in the deserted buildings near the river's banks, and from here and the roads leading to the bridge they poured volley after volley on the enemy.

As soon as the last gunner had fallen a squadron of French horse, emerging from the cover of a neighbouring house, dashed at the gum, hoping to reach and spike it before assistance arrived. In this they were foiled by the bravery of the British officers in command; but in the hand-to-hand combat that followed, fully half of the bridge's defenders were cut down. The Chasseurs lost two of their men and drew back; then, reinforced by the arrival of the infantry, they charged once more and swept the enemy from the field.

> "At the bridge over the Castlebar River a horrible crush ensued. The main body of the British army had converged to that point, and the narrow structure was blocked with field guns, caissons and supply wagons, against which the struggling mass of humanity surged in unreasoning terror. Here it was everyone for himself, the alternative to the luckless foot soldier being death under the hoof or a plunge into the waters beneath. To increase the confusion some shots fell in among the fugitives, and in their desperation, they turned their weapons against each other. How many perished on the bridge has never been fully ascertained, but for weeks afterward the river and the lough nearby threw up mutilated corpses in the uniform of the British line and of the Anglo-Irish yeomanry."
>
> Finns Leinster Journal - Saturday 29 September 1798

While the braver elements of the British army at Castlebar attempted to stem the rout and many were prepared to die rather than flee for their lives, the same could not be said of the majority who sped along the road south to Hollymount and Tuam, both garrison towns. Some were so scared that their continued on their flight until they reached Athlone.

This rout has passed into history as "The Races of Castlebar."

The fighting had lasted just six hours from 6 am until midday and when it was finally over and the last enemy troops had been dislodged from the town, the French could finally take stock of their situation. They had won a stunning victory.

5 Fatal Delay in Castlebar

True, their losses were considerable but with less than 800 trained soldiers behind him, Humbert had beaten two experienced English generals, Lake and Hutchinson, along with upwards of 6,00 soldiers and militia.

After their initial charge at the English artillery positions and the devastating reply to their advance, the Irish are said to have taken no further part in the fighting but there are local contemporary accounts that contradict this. Thomas Pakenham, the noted historian, described the behaviour of the English at this battle as one of the most ignominious defeats in British military history and few would disagree with him.

Then something truly incongruous happened. The French officers decided to relieve stress by having a ball.

Sir Jonah Barrington, a prominent Irish judge and historian, described what happened next in his memoirs.

> *"Despite the hardships of their march to the field of victory, despite their decimation by shot and shell, the soldiers of the French Republic, once the conflict over, had thoughts but for distraction and pleasure, The Gallic nature, with its fantastic mobility, its violent*

contrasts, once more asserted itself. On the very evening of the battle, with the dead lying unburied on every side, with the unhoused wounded torturing the air with their moans, Humbert's officers brushed off the dust and powder of the fray and assembled all that remained of youth and beauty "to trip the light fantastic toe" from "eve till dewy morn." It was a strange scene, the large, bare hall, lighted by the mellow gleam of flickering candles; the officers in their shabby uniforms, some embellished with white bandages that would later blush with the blood of the wounds they concealed; the lithesome Irish belles in their bucolic finery, whose simple minds were half repelled. by these rough exteriors, half frightened at this reckless indifference to surrounding dangers and hardships, yet wholly fascinated by the martial halo that enveloped their " deliverers."

The faint, wheezy notes of a spinet, accompanied by the screech of a fiddle manipulated by fingers more used to grasping a sword than a bow, supplied the music that wooed the too-willing feet to merry measures. Through the open casements the night air, still heavy with the breath of battle, entered.to cool the hot checks of the damsels, and by its familiar odor to spur on the sons of Mars to softer conquests."

The time had now come for Humbert to reward his officers who had distinguished themselves on the battlefield and this he did before the night was over. Sarrazin, already raised one grade at Killala, was now a general of division; Fontaine, who had led the cavalry with such decisive results, became a general of brigade; and chiefs of battalion Ardouin, Aremare, and. Dufour were now brigade commanders. Every man, in fact, who had at all distinguished himself during the day and there were few who had not, received his reward that night.

There were widespread celebrations throughout the region as the news of the French victory spread throughout the neighbourhood.

Bonfires blazed from every hill around Castlebar, and out towards Westport and Newport to the west. At Westport some acts of vandalism were committed on Protestant property, but the owners were able to flee to Castlebar and find protection from Humbert, of all people. However, the ancestral home of Lord Altamount was amongst the properties looted as was the house of his brother, Denis Browne. The latter was to exact a terrible revenge.

Denis Browne was High Sheriff of Mayo at the time the insurrection was put down and using his powers he hunted down rebels and those suspected of having French sympathies and he had scores hanged, whipped, transported or press ganged into the Royal Navy or military regiments.

The Last Invasion of Ireland

By the following morning, the 28th, the town was overflowing with peasants from all parts of the province. Some were armed with rusty match-locks, some with pikes, and all had some form of basic weapons. Excitement ran high and every one of them wanted to side with Humbert.

Those who did not come to join for active service came loaded with gifts of meat, butter, poultry, eggs, fish, etc., for the troops. One party came with a steer that had been cooked in a quarry near the town on heated slabs of limestone, a custom dating back to Hannibal's time. Gifts of clothing and footwear donated by merchants from Castlebar and the nearby towns also arrived. Drilling the raw recruits and getting them accustomed to the French muskets, swords and small arms took up some valuable time.

A large contingent came from the Newport-Ballycroy area. A company from Ballycroy and Erris had previously marched to Ballina to join. A body of insurgents from Westport and Louisburgh included two Augustinian Friars, Fr. Myles Prendergast and Fr. Michael Gannon. This force was led by Johnny Gibbons, locally nicknamed Johnny the Outlaw

From the Knock-Aughamore district came two strong companies under

Captain Seamas O'Malley and Richard Jordan. A company of recruits came from Killedan and Bohola parishes under Henry Valentine Jordan of Rosslevin.

A large company from the glens around Nephin Mountain who joined on the route from Ballina to Castlebar was led by Captain Peadar Jordan of Coolnabinna.

History as It Happened

Jordan escaped to Achill Island after the collapse of the rising and died suddenly while on the run there. He composed the poem, "Cúl na Binn," one of the finest poems of the '98 period.

Another local leader who joined the Franco-Irish force just before the fight for Castlebar with a strong body of pikemen was Captain Willie Mangan of Sion Hill.

The first rout of any of the Redcoat regiments guarding the approaches to the town took place at Sion Hill, according to local tradition.

As always, Humbert opposed all attempts to vandalise and loot the property of loyalists. He was unable to prevent the pillage of the residences of Lords Lucan and Altamont. Taking advantage of the confusion caused by the capture of Castlebar, the insurgents ransacked these two magnificent mansions from attic to cellar. Lord Altamont's property suffered most. His horses and cattle were driven off, his wine casks emptied, and his furniture smashed during the drunken looters. The carved doors were dragged from their hinges, and the stained-glass window panes shattered to pieces.

The French officers had great difficulty in restraining groups of half-intoxicated rebels from creating further damage and for a while there were genuine fears that there would be a massacre of Protestants in the town.

In "Memoirs of the various rebellions in Ireland," Sir Richard Musgrave wrote:

"Another inhabitant of Castlebar has left an interesting account of the arrival at his house of a party of the invaders. He obtained their good will by supplying them with meat and wine. The rebels," he writes, "who accompanied them at first, plundered us of various articles; but one day when they revisited. us I alarmed my foreign visitors, who expelled and chastised them severely. One of them, by name Phillip Sheers, was from Holland; I gave him my watch, but he kindly returned it; another, Bartholomew Baille, from Paris, was mild, learned, and rather silent. He had been a priest, but on the overthrow of his order became a soldier. He denied a future existence. One Ballisceoy, a Spaniard, was as intrepid as Hannibal. Since the age of fifteen he had followed the profession of a soldier. He had been a prisoner in Prussia, in Paris, and in London. He had. been confined in a dungeon at Constantinople. He had crossed the Alps with Bonaparte and fought under him in Italy. His body, head and face were covered with wounds. He was a hard drinker, a great swearer, and mocked religion; and yet he was very fond of children, and never entered my apartment without constantly enquiring for my wife, who was on the point of lying-in. The fourth was from Rochelle and the fifth from Toulon."

Humbert committed a grave mistake at this time.

Having been sure-footed and incisive in his planning so far, he now miscalculated badly. Instead of pressing home his advantage while the enemy were in a total state of disarray, he decided to stay on in Castlebar instead of advancing eastwards to the midlands where he had been told there would be a large body of United Irishmen waiting to join him.

On August 31, four days after the entrance of the French into Castlebar, a new civil government was proclaimed for the entire province. The governing body was to consist of twelve members, to be named by the French commander, with one prominent Catholic, John Moore, as president. The town of Castlebar would be the seat of government. The first duty of the executive, as defined. by the proclamation, was the organisation and equipping of a force of militia and the furnishing of supplies to the French and their allies. The force to be created was to number eight regiments of infantry of 1,200 men each, and four regiments of cavalry of 600 men each.

All persons having received arms or clothing and failing to join the army within twenty-four hours were declared "rebels and traitors." The closing paragraph of the proclamation required, "....in the English, whose destruction alone can insure the independence and welfare of Ancient Hibernia!"

As he knew full well already, the men who would probably man his army were likely to be as indisciplined and incorrigible as those who had already flocked to join him so the idea of leaving it to someone else to wield them into an efficient army was preposterous.

He must also have realised that the British were going to launch a full-scale attack on the town to recapture it and that he would not have the resources to withstand such an assault.

His only hope lay in getting to Granard in Westmeath and securing reinforcements before the net closed on him and his little army.

He knew his men badly needed some time to rest and recuperate and he needed to requisition some supplies and horses, but every hour was going to be precious as he was very much aware.

He should also have known that the time and effort his officers spent in trying to make soldiers out of his new recruits was not going to be worth the time and effort required. Since very few of the rebels had any idea of where they were going or what was likely to lie in store for them, they spent their time drinking and looting or attempting to do so.

One or two days at most should have been enough for him to look after his most pressing needs but instead he tarried until September 3rd before leaving, once again at nightfall.

He had taken the town on the 27th of August and he had waited until September 3rd to depart and this delay was going to be fatal for his plans.

As far as Humbert was therefore concerned, everything pointed towards a rapid advance in the direction of Granard and once he set out, his enemies would be able to guess what his intentions were. But here already the results of delay were becoming clear. He was informed that Lord Comwallis had arrived at Athlone with a large body of regulars and he knew other hostile armies were preparing to block his progress further south or east. Having learned from a spy that counties Sligo and. Leitrim were comparatively free from the enemy, he decided to adopt that roundabout route to the capital. He had already sent orders to the troops he had left at Killala, and a small detachment stationed at Ballina, to meet him en route,

6 The Long March

On the night of September 3, the first division of his army with the baggage and cannon set out for Sligo. The next morning the second division followed, about 400 Frenchmen and from 1,500 to 2,000 Irish auxiliaries. The majority of the "patriots" had preferred remaining behind and, in truth, he was not sorry to see the last of them.

By September 3, he had realised that he would not get assistance from France, which probably had been another reason for his delay in getting away before the hostile forces converging on Castlebar would encircle the town. This was yet another reason to abandon Castlebar.

He passed through Swinford where his army stopped to eat, the food was supplied by the local people, and they continued on to Bellaghy. By now his Irish recruits were thoroughly fed up with the incessant forced marching, continual rain and the continual sniping by the detachments of the local militia who harassed any section of Humbert's men when they separated from the main body.

He was confronted by an English force, roughly the same size as his own, which had come out from Sligo to confront him and in a sharp encounter at Carrignagat he defeated them but decided not to march on to Sligo as intended but to swing right

The Last Invasion of Ireland

and cross the Shannon into north Longford at the bridge of Ballintra which scouts informed him was not guarded.

On the 25th of that month, the staunchly loyalist newspaper, Belfast Telegraph, printed the following uncomplimentary account of his progress since leaving Castlebar:

> *"Awed by The Approach of the army under command of his excellency the Lord Lieutenant, the French after having been 7 days in on the undisturbed possession of Castlebar made a precipitate retreat from thence about one o'clock in the morning of Tuesday the 4th instant and barely halted until they arrived at Tubbercurry where they surprised a vidette post, the Liney troop of cavalry commanded by Charles O'Hara, Esq., taking Harlow Knott Esq. prisoner, whose only son was killed in the onset.*
>
> Early in the day they arrived at Collooney, spreading themselves down to Carricknagat, on the mountains, behind walls and ditches etc. About 11 in the morning, Col. Vereker of the Limerick militia, marched hence against them with detachments of the following corps, viz. City of Limerick militia, 220-Essex fencibles, 20- Loyal Sligo infantry,20- Ballimore infantry, 10- Drumcliff infantry, 16- together with detachments from the Tyerill, Lincy and Drumcliff troops of yeomen cavalry, and only two curricle guns- the whole not forming a force equal to one-tenth of that engaged and highly appointed against them."

History as It Happened

(Humbert had at most 800 French soldiers and roughly 1,500 Irishmen tagging along behind him.) Richard Musgrave, (Memoirs of Irish Rebellions) described the French departure from Castlebar and the first stage of their journey in the following words:

> *"The French at their departure from Castlebar were about nine hundred, including officers and they had a great mob of rebels…They did not halt until they reached Barley-field, the seat of Mr. M'Manus, whither some of the French officers went to order provisions to be sent thence for their use to Swineford.*

They arrived there about seven in the evening, halted for about two hours, and refreshed the troops. General Humbert continued all the time in the field, where he ate his dinner, which had been dressed at the house of Mr. Brabazon."

When the army reached Swinford, the men were turned into a field where the former vocational school was later to be built and there, they had dinner. Four steers, the property of the local landlord, Sir Anthony Brabazon, were hastily prepared and roasted on four large iron gates that had been brought along for this purpose from the M'Manus estate. Humbert and his high-ranking officers dined at Corley's Hotel in The Square.

Some of the local men, led by Seamus Dubh Horkan from, the townland of Rathscanlon, joined the march as the Franco-Irish army set out on the next stage of their journey to Bellaghy just across the border with County Sligo. They camped for the night in a field between Ballaghy and the hamlet of Tubbercurry, several miles further north.

It seems that they decided to stay in an orchard where the apple crop wasn't fully ripe. The starving marchers couldn't resist the temptation to devour them all, but they did so with disastrous results. By the following morning many were in no fit state to confront Colonel Veredeker and his troops who had advanced south from Sligo as far as Collooney to block their path as they were afflicted with severe diarrhoea.

As the march proceeded, new recruits came forward to join Humbert but this recruitment was balanced by desertion of others who had joined earlier but who by now had enough forced marching and continual fighting and who dropped out in ever increasing numbers until the French felt obliged to position guards at the rear and on each flank of the marching column to prevent this. Besides, meals of beef were rare enough, the staple food was bustán, a mixture of oatmeal and milk that could be rolled and pressed into rolls or cakes.

In the conflict against Vereker, both Humbert and his adversary each miscalculated the numerical strength of the other with the result that there was no close hand to hand fighting, neither wishing to advance too far from the safety of his entrenched position.

An act of outstanding bravery by Bartholomew Teeling eventually broke the stalemate and caused Vereker to retreat, leaving the way open for Humbert to veer right and head for Dromahair in Leitrim.

A lone English cannon was wreaking havoc on the French until Teeling mounted his horse and charged at the gun.

Following a zigzag course, he managed to get close enough to the gunner to shoot him dead before returning safely to his comrades. It's not clear why Vereker decided to retreat when the gun was silenced but he did so and instead of returning to Sligo, he fell back to Ballyshannon.

Humbert meanwhile found an unguarded bridge across the Shannon at Ballintra and got his men across safely but failed to blow up the bridge when all were on the eastern side. Fontaine, who was given the task of destroying the structure was not able to do so because of a lack of gunpowder and Lake's men following closely behind were able to repair the damage by using the stones from a nearby house that they knocked down.

All the while Humbert's men were under severe harassment by Lake's advance party. Most if not all of his Irish auxiliaries would have taken the opportunity to drop out if only they had a chance to do so. But from reports they were getting of Lake's merciless treatment of any stragglers that were unlucky enough to fall into his hands, they had no choice but to keep on marching.

Gribayedoff described the conduct of General Lake and his men who were harassing Humbert's army from the rear:

> *"General Lake, in compliance with the lord-lieutenant's instructions, was meanwhile pressing close on the rear of Humbert's army. From Ballyhadireen he marched on the afternoon of the 5th with his combined forces to Ballahy, through which place he learned the French had passed the preceding evening at*

about seven o'clock. He marched onward without further delay and entered Tubbercury at seven. He found Colonel Crawford awaiting him here with the Hompeschers and the Roxburgh Fencible Cavalry, and henceforth this detachment acted as the advance guard of the army. The services they rendered in harassing the French were invaluable, but their course was marked by the most revolting acts of barbarity. They took no prisoners under any circumstances but cut down in cold blood all stragglers from Humbert's Irish contingent, and even entire bodies of the rebels who offered to surrender. Thus for miles and miles the road in the wake of the French army was strewn with the dead and dying, farm-houses and private dwellings in the vicinity were reduced to ashes, and devastation was spread all over a lately prosperous country. When the British force reached Collooney, whence Humbert had departed a short while before, a number of wounded French were discovered in a barn under the care of a surgeon. These experienced good treatment; but a Longford deserter who fell into the hands of the Hompeschers received short shrift, and his body, riddled with bullets, was marched over by the entire army."

After crossing the river, Humbert turned southwards, hoping to join up with the United Irishmen he was expecting to meet at Granard in Westmeath. At Cloone in south Leitrim he was forced to stop to give his men a couple of hours rest. He had given orders that he and his officers should be awakened after two hours but for some reason the guard let them sleep on for another two hours. This delay made all the difference between getting to Granard and being encircled by an enemy pincer movement. He was finally halted at Ballinamuck in north Longford within a few miles of his destination.

The epic march had come to an end

7 The Massacre of Ballinamuck

Seeing that he had no other option, Humbert ordered a halt and lined his men up in battle formation. The place of his last stand was Shanmullagh Hill, a little promontory in the townland of Ballinamuck.

His left was partly protected by a bog, and his right by another bog and a lake. All in all, he picked the most advantageous position to be found for miles around but the sheer overwhelming superiority of men and resources that the English had meant that Humbert and his army had no hope of getting to Granard and the reinforcements he had hoped to meet there.

He was stopped just four miles short of where he wanted to go but that made no difference to their plight as they looked around them on Shanmullagh Hill.

Humbert made it clear to his men that he had no intention of surrendering.

But just as hostilities were about to commence, something dramatic happened that caught the encircled Franco-Irish force completely off-guard. Without warning and without telling anyone else, Sarrazin, Humbert's able second in command through the campaign so far, decided to surrender. He put his cap on the point of his sword as a recognised token of surrender and held it aloft. At this sight, his division of 200 men also laid down their weapons and followed his lead.

Two officers on the English side on seeing this rode forward and a trumpet sounded. Sarrazin ordered a French trumpeter to respond and formally acknowledge is capitulation. On behalf of General Lake, the pair of horsemen demanded the immediate surrender of the French army but Sarrazin replied that he did not have the authority to do so and said that the demand must be relayed to its commander-in-chief, General Humbert.

While the parley with Sarrazin was taking place, General Lake was mistakenly informed that the French army were going to surrender, and Lake sent two officers forward to Humbert's position to accept his sword.

To their great surprise, they were met with a hail of musket fire and one of the officers, Major-General Craddock, was shot in the shoulder.

Now the battle commenced. Lake sent a body of infantry to outflank Humbert's left flank, but Humbert drew his men back to another hill a little further away. The British artillery unit was brought forward but Lake saw a large body of pikemen being assembled to mount an attack on the guns as had happened at Castlebar. He positioned a body of infantry, flanked by a cavalry division to protect his cannon and prevent another Irish attack. Humbert had posted a body of tirailleurs, light infantry, and some cannon and they were causing considerable losses to the enemy's right flank. Lake himself rode too close to this scene of combat and nearly lost his life as a bullet grazed his shoulder.

Every tirailleur fought to the end but eventually all were either killed, wounded or captured and the guns were silenced.

Throughout the course of conflict, Humbert was unwilling to accept surrender and fought alongside his men, sword in hand. He almost lost his life when an English dragoon knocked him from his saddle and bore down on him intending to run him through. His aide-de-camp, Bartholomew Teeling, came to his rescue.

At this, Humbert and his officers realised that they had no hope of winning and to save further loss of life, they ordered resistance to cease.

After a half hour of intense fighting, the battle of Ballinamuck had ended. As far as the French were concerned the battle was over. But now the most tragic act in the drama was to be played.

The unfortunate rebels, who still numbered several hundreds, expecting no quarter, fought for their lives. They were forced into a bog where they were surrounded by horse, foot and artillery. Raked with cross-fire from all points, sabred by the horsemen and bayoneted by the infantry, there remained only a skeleton of the solid column that had stood side by side with Humbert's troops at the beginning of the battle; and those who finally were allowed to lay down their arms only exchanged the bullet or sword for the rope. This is what one eye-witness wrote:

> *"We pursued the rebels through the bog. the country was covered for miles around with their slain. We remained for a few days burying the dead, hung General Blake and nine of the Longford militias; we brought one hundred and*

History as It Happened

thirteen prisoners to Carrick-on-Shannon, nineteen of whom we executed in one day, and left the remainder for others to follow our example"

The treatment of the French prisoners by the British military authorities was exceptionally generous. The officers were entertained at a sumptuous banquet at Longford.

The prisoners were sent to Dublin by the Grand Canal on six large horse-drawn barges. Their journey lasted nearly a week. The first one carried the escort of Fermanagh militia with a full military band, the second one the captive officers, and the remainder transported the rank and file. Nothing, according to contemporary accounts, could dampen the spirits of the captives. They were constantly gathering in groups, playing cards, dancing, and above all, singing the Marseillaise.

From Dublin, they were transported to the port of Liverpool and at their arrival an immense, friendly crowd gathered to greet them. At Litchfield, where the officers were temporarily quartered, General Humbert was visited by a deputation of clergymen, headed by a brother of Cornwallis, who expressed their gratitude for the protection extended by him to the Protestants of Mayo.

Humbert's first request to the British authorities was that his Irish officers receive considerate treatment, but he insisted on immunity for those who had come over from France and who held commissions in the French army. He was particularly solicitous about Bartholomew Teeling, his aide-de-camp. Teeling's brother wrote later: "After the surrender of the

French army a cartel was concluded for the exchange of prisoners, under which General Humbert, with the residue of his forces, was to proceed to France. The most bitter regret was evinced by the French general in finding that Teeling was not to derive the benefit of this arrangement. The latter had surrendered when his general was captured. He was easily identified by General Lake due to his recent exploits on the long march. It was said that several British officers had recognised him first but were not going to betray his presence until he was spotted by Lake.

On taking muster of the French officers he was set apart and claimed as a British subject by General Lake. Humbert remonstrated; he demanded his officer in the name of the French Government and claimed that his arrest was a breach of national honour and of the law of arms.

"I will not part with him,' he exclaimed with violent emotion. I will accompany him to prison or to death." He did accompany his aide-de-camp to Longford prison, where he remained until the following day, when the French prisoners were conveyed to the capital, and thence embarked with the least possible delay on board transports for England.

Teeling was brought to Dublin to be tried by court-martial. Matthew Tone, who had been arrested the day after the battle, was also recognized as an Irishman and returned for trial.

Teeling was put on trial for high treason less than two weeks after his capture, and, notwithstanding the many character references from his enemies and praise from all quarters for his kindness to loyal prisoners and his strict observance of the rules of civilised warfare, he was condemned to death as a traitor to his country.

Humbert, on board the Van Tromp, a prison ship, wrote a touching letter of appeal to the president of the court-martial two days before the commencement of the trial.

This, in part, is what Humbert had to say about his aide-de-com when he wrote the appeal:

"Teeling, by his bravery and generous conduct, has prevented in all the towns through which we have passed the insurgents from proceeding to the most criminal excesses. Write to Killala, to Ballina, to Castlebar; there does not live an inhabitant who will not render him the greatest justice. This officer is commissioned by my government; and all these considerations, joined to his gallant conduct toward your people, ought to impress much in his favour. I flatter myself that the proceedings in your court will be favorable to him, and that you will treat him with the greatest indulgence."

Lord Cornwallis turned a deaf ear to all appeals for clemency on the unfortunate man's behalf, and on the morning of September 24th he was led to the gallows erected on Arbour Hill. He was attired in full regimentals of a French staff officer. He wore a large French cocked hat, with a gold loop and button and the tricolor cockade, blue surtout-coat and blue pantaloons and half boots.

Around his neck was a white cravat, encircled by a black stock, very full and projecting, which the executioner removed in order to adjust the noose. The forty minutes that elapsed. between the doomed man's arrival under the fatal beam and. the completion of the hangman's task he passed in conversation with Brigade-Major Sandes, and until the very last, no tremor was perceptible in his voice. Matthew Tone, Theobald's brother, suffered death in a similar manner a few days afterwards.

8 The Second Battle of Castlebar

The surrender of Humbert's "Army of Ireland" at Ballinamuck was catastrophic in every way for the long-suffering Catholic population of Mayo and the province of Connacht as a whole but the bloodshed did not end at that.

The Irish rebels who held Killala and Ballina after Humbert's departure for Castlebar remained defiant to the end. All hope may have been gone and they knew well what their fate was likely to be as the English concentrated their forces for a final push against rebel positions, but they contested every yard of ground from the ford at Foxford back to Downpatrick Head, several miles north of Killala, where the last of them were cornered.

Castlebar was re-occupied by the English army three days after the French and their Irish allies set out on their doomed march to the east.

Barely three days after the surrender of Humbert and the ending of the brief illusion of liberty and freedom, 2,000 of those who had remained behind left Ballina under the leadership of Major O'Kane and Patrick Barrett, a former member of the local militia, set out from Killala to retake Castlebar.

In the early dawn of September 12, two citizens of the town, Edward Mayley and John Dudgeon, while stationed on lookout in the northern suburbs, heard the thud of horses' hooves approaching from the direction of Barnageeha, and presently saw two horsemen riding at a furious pace. The sentinels blocked their way and demanded to know who they were and where they were going.

The strangers happened to be advance scouts for the advancing rebel army and were careless enough to blurt out their mission to the pair of armed strangers who had confronted them. They were taken aback when they had pistols pointed at them and were ordered to dismount and were disarmed on the spot.

The two rebels, who had evidently mistaken their adversaries for friends, surrendered were taken as prisoners into the town, where their captors raised the alarm.

It was fortunate for the Protestant population that the proposed attack had been discovered and the defenders were able to get into some sort of formation to repel the expected attack.

The main body occupied the market cross, commanding the principal avenues, with the only piece of cannon in town; another division was posted between the market-house and one of the town gates; and a third was stationed at the north end, where the rebels were expected to make their main attack. By seven o'clock the attackers had concentrated their forces near the north entrance and opened a heavy fire of musketry on the town. The fire was returned by the Highlanders who were stationed in the town as they had picked out strong defensive

History as It Happened

positions beforehand, whereas O'Kane's men were exposed to the enemy fire as they had to leave any sort of cover behind as they mounted an attack.

The soldiers, being under cover, experienced little or no loss, while their opponents were picked off by the dozen. Seeing this, Major O'Kane formed a column of assault and made a dash forward, in an attempt to overrun the enemy position. The fighting was frenzied for some time and the outcome remained very much in doubt but whereas the majority of the attackers were only armed with the most basic of weapons, such as rusty matchlocks and crude pikes their opponents were trained soldiers and experienced at hand to hand fighting.

Gradually the attack lost impetus and when a small detachment of townspeople on horseback arrived on the scene and charged at the rebels, the latter faltered and then scattered in all directions. An example of the Races of Castlebar in reverse.

Scores of fleeing rebels were either shot or cut down by the cavalry or compelled to surrender. Had the two advance scouts not been so careless and blurted out the news that an attack was imminent to the sentinels on the lookout earlier that day, there is little doubt that the rebels would have overrun the town.

More than likely, there would have been widespread looting and arson and without a doubt, many of the inhabitants of Castlebar would have been massacred.

Inevitably, that in turn would have led to even harsher reprisals when the English forces did return to Mayo to restore order. The bloodiest month in Mayo's history would have even bloodier.

> *Extract of a letter from Castlebar, Sept. 12.*
> *"Early this morning, Mr. Higgins, reconnoitering the neighbourhood, discovered the Rebels in force, which he communicated to Captain Urquhart, of Frazer's fencibles, and immediately ordered his men and our yeomanry, whom he posted in the best manner possible. At eight o'clock we were attacked by upwards of 400, and after a short, but smart action, they ran, leaving many of their killed and wounded. Captain Urquhart ordered the Castlebar and Tyrawley cavalry, under Luke Higgins, Esq. acting Captain of the Castlebar troop, to pursue then, which they did in a spirited manner for some miles and have just returned with several prisoners. You will be happy to hear that we did not lose a man,"*

Freemans Journal,

9 The French Officers in Killala

When the two hundred French infantry withdrew from Killala, at the beginning of September, to reinforce the main army at Castlebar, only two officers, Lieutenant-Colonel Charost and Captain Ponson remained in the town; and they were joined later by Captain Boudet, who had been stationed in Westport but had to withdraw from the town in the face of the advance of a loyal detachment. These three men probably saved the Protestant population from destruction.

Charost himself was a man of charming and sympathetic personality. He soon earned the respect of Protestants and Catholics alike.

He told the bishop that his father being a Catholic and his mother a Protestant, they had left him the liberty of choosing for himself and he had never yet found time to think about it and, until Heaven should grant him repose, he wouldn't make such a decision. But he was very sure that while he lived in this world it was his duty to do all the good to his fellow-creatures that he could.

In his memoirs, Bishop Stock gave him credit for respecting the beliefs of others and taking great care that the divine services of the Protestants at Killala Castle were not be disturbed in any way.

Ponson and Boudet, according to the bishop, were each interesting in his own way but lacked some of the sterling qualities of their superior. Ponson was a curious little man, not exceeding five feet six inches but extremely courageous and, in temperament being in command came naturally to him. This was just as well as the rebels were growing desperate for prey and destruction.

He was always ready to confront the marauders, whom, if he caught them in the act of disobeying orders and breaching discipline, he belaboured them without mercy and without any fear for his own safety. In the words of Bishop Stock; "He was strictly honest and could not bear the want of this quality in others; so that his patience was pretty well tried by his Irish allies, for whom he could not find names sufficiently expressive of contempt."

Stock wrote of Boudet:

"In startling contrast to Ponson, Boudet was a man six feet two inches in height. In person, complexion and gravity, he was no inadequate representation of the Knight of Ia Manche, whose example he followed in a recital of his own prowess and wonderful exploits, delivered. in measured. language and an imposing seriousness of aspect. His manner, however, though distant was polite, and he seemed. possessed of more than common share of feeling, if a judgment might be formed from the energy with which he declaimed on the miseries of wars and revolutions. His integrity and

> *courage appeared unquestionable. On the whole, when we became familiarised to his failings, we saw every reason to respect his virtues."*

However, the bishop did not speak highly of Truc, the French officer left at Ballina. He denounced him as a man of evil disposition, lacking both in common honesty and courage." Truc shared authority with O'Kane and both were under the orders of Charost.

Charost's' first problem after the departure of Humbert for the front was maintaining the security of the large district entrusted to him as it covered many square miles of rugged country, a long seaboard and the towns of Killala and Ballina. This whole area was swarming with the armed bands of insurgents who had remained behind for the purpose of plundering the Protestant landholders rather than joining the French in the field. There were several thousands of them and because of their unrest and lawlessness a strong guard at first nightly patrolled the town of Killala and its suburbs; but this measure wasn't enough to keep the mob under control so Charost decided to arm the townspeople who were well-disposed to law an order.

By special proclamation Catholics and Protestants were offered arms and ammunition, with no other condition than the promise of returning them on demand. The offer was eagerly accepted by Protestants and Catholics alike, but the result was a failure.

From the very first the insurgents under command protested that the weapons could surely be used against themselves. The protestations soon turned into threats, which intimidated some of the Protestants that they returned the arms shortly after they had received them. The insurgents, not satisfied with this, adopted, on the few following days, the tactics of harassing the loyalist minority with house searches, under the pretence of searching for concealed weapons.

The harassed victims of this intimidation begged Charost to call in the weapons he had given out and restrict their use to those who had joined the French army. So, he had to find another way to keep the situation under control and halt the attacks on the entire community.

As Humbert had done in Castlebar, he issued a proclamation some days later, establishing a provisional government over the district within his care. He divided it into departments; each presided over by a magistrate, with an armed guard of sixteen or twenty men. None of these were required to declare themselves either for or against the king, being simply considered civil officers engaged in the service of keeping the peace. Mr. James Devitt, "a substantial Roman Catholic tradesman of good sense and moderation," was unanimously elected civil magistrate for Killala, and thenceforth the town was regularly policed 'by three bodies of fifty men each, all standing directly under his orders.

10 Anarchy in Killala

However, even at that, tension still remained as some turned their attention to the bishop's palace, where, in addition to his family, the three French officers were housed. Few dwellings offered more temptations than his, for besides his own property it contained many valuables deposited in his keeping by the Protestant community when the French arrived. For the defence of the castle a guard about twenty strong was drawn from the garrison.

The men were relieved once in twenty-four hours, but even they constituted a poor guarantee for the security of the household as they all regarded those Protestant possessions as being rightfully theirs. At times the situation was most alarming, and only the tact and nerve of the commandant averted the threatened breakdown in law and order.

On one occasion a drunken troublemaker named Toby Flannagan, who had promoted himself to the rank of major, arrested a man named. Goodwin, for no other reason than that he was a Protestant.

Word of the affair was brought to Charost while he engaged in a game of piquet at the castle, and immediately the whole party repaired to the scene of the trouble. They found the "major" mounted on his charger, drunk and vociferous, surrounded by an admiring mob.

Flannagan refused to release the prisoner as Charost had ordered him to do. This was a critical moment. Failure to enforce his authority would have led to a total collapse of law and order. Charost immediately ordered Flannagan to dismount. There was a ring of determination in his voice that brooked no delay. The culprit looked at his adherents for support, and finding none, he sullenly obeyed. Charost walked over to him and disarmed him and then and sent him under a guard of his own followers to the very jail where he had sent his victim. This incident finished Flannagan's martial career.

At Ballina, thanks to the indifference or connivance of Truc, the insurgents were able to do very much as they pleased. Father Owen Cowley, of Castleconnor, was their leader.

Being fluent in French he soon won the confidence of Truc and soon possessed almost unlimited authority over the town and its environs. On the pretence of securing the young republic against the plotting of inside enemies, Cowley sent out bands of armed insurgents to arrest and bring to town the Protestant farmers of the neighborhood; and in a few days over sixty of these people, after seeing their houses demolished, were committed to a temporary jail in the house of Colonel Henry King. Having made sure of his prey, Cowley's next step was to gain permission to destroy them, but here he found unexpected opposition from O'Kane and Barrett.

Suspecting the priest's designs, Barrett interrogated him, and was haughtily told that Truc had given orders for the execution of the prisoners. Barrett flew to the chief, and through an interpreter laid the matter before him. They soon realised that Cowley had lied, a fact that Barrett took good care to accuse him of in the most public manner. Barrett's temerity, however, nearly cost him his life, for while he was still speaking one of the priest's followers made a hinge at him with a pike, and only his quick retreat saved him from the fury of the bloodthirsty mob.

Cowley's methods and intentions remained unchanged.

On the night of September 8th, about twelve o'clock, he entered the improvised jail to gloat over his victims. They were packed together like sheep, in a room scarcely large enough to hold half their number. Realising that in the general confusion some of the prisoners he had arrested might be Catholics, he greeted them with the words: "Lie down, Orange; rise up, Croppy." Although the nominal head of almost all Mayo, Charost's personal influence was limited to the immediate vicinity of Killala.

One of the prisoners, noticed the speaker's clerical garb and approached him with a request for protection, but all he got was a stunning blow over the head with a heavy cudgel. Cowley worked himself into a passion, and shaking his fist at the unfortunate prisoners, he roared: "You parcel of heretics have no more religion than a parcel of pigs. I do not know whether you will be put to death before ten o'clock to-morrow by being burned with barrels of tar, or by pikes, or by musket balls!"

The priest's intentions were happily not carried out, for when Charost's attention was called to the danger of the Protestants; he came in person to Ballina, and reprimanded

Truc severely for listening to accusations on the score of religion. He ordered all persons arrested by Cowley's henchmen to be brought before him and spent a full day examining them and discharged every one of them. The prisoners were free to return to their homes. To many that word meant but a heap of ashes."

During this period of wide scale looting and general unrest in the Killala region, several country houses, homes of prominent Protestants, were ransacked and their contents destroyed. A Presbyterian meeting-house between Killala and Ballina was attacked and razed to the ground.

News of these various outrages having been brought to Killala, Charost despatched Bondet and Edwin Stock, one of the bishop's sons, to Summerhill to appease the mob, and another party of men to Castlereagh to save what remained of the provisions and liquors. The appearance of the emissaries ended the siege at Mr. Bourke's house but the Castlereagh party, which consisted entirely of natives, could think of no better expedient for preserving the spirits from the thirsty bandits that coveted them than by concealing as much as they could in their own stomachs. The consequence was that they returned to Killala extremely drunk!

Charost's indignation at such barbarity knew no bounds. He told the insurgents that he was a Chef de Brigade, not a Chef de Brigands, and declared that if he ever caught them preparing to despoil and murder Protestants, he would side with the latter to "the very last extremity."

Meanwhile, all in Killala, rebels and loyalists, were anxiously awaiting news from the front as Humbert and his little army progressed eastwards. The tension was palpable.

11 The End of the Rebellion

Contradictory rumours were constantly circulating, and it was not until September 19, the day of O'Kane's attack on Castlebar, that some definite information reached Charost of the capitulation of Humbert's force at Ballinamuck. He realised that a crisis was approaching for he was aware of the mood of the insurgents and he feared they would massacre every Protestant in town. He decided to do nothing further than attempting to preserve law and order in his area of command until the arrival of a regular British force and then he and his companions could surrender without discredit.

In pursuance of this in the apartments occupied by the three officers, twelve loaded carbines were kept in readiness, and among the seven or eight trusted members of the bishop's household a variety of weapons were distributed.

Henceforth the Frenchmen remained constantly on the alert, watching not only all newcomers and applicants the castle gate, but also their own guard of twenty men. The precautions were necessary.

Day by day the prospect grew more threatening. On September 18th, news of General Trench's preparations to march against them from Castlebar caused the insurgent leaders to send in a demand to Charost that the Protestants be imprisoned in the cathedral as hostages.

This he flatly refused to do.

The next day an angry crowd gathered about the castle gate, complaining that their friends and relations in Castlebar were being ill-treated by the British. To quieten them the bishop suggested that two emissaries be sent to General Trench to entreat him to do nothing to his prisoners that would provoke reprisals on the Protestants at Killala. The proposition met with immediate approval. Roger Maguire, son of a Crossmolina brewer, and Dean Thompson, who with his family had occupied the bishop's apartments since the appearance of the French, were selected for the mission. Early the following morning they started out on their journey.

A false report that the English were approaching unsettled the inhabitants, Catholics and Protestants alike. Rioting and drunkenness became widespread.

Later that day the commandant, by his presence of mind, averted another danger. Just as he was sitting down to dine; word was brought to him that a party of angry pikemen had assembled outside the castle, bent on plunder. Charost walked out leisurely, accompanied by his two companions and found them preparing to batter in the gates.

In his ordinary tone of command, he called "attention," divided them into platoons, and proceeded to put them through their daily exercise. His nonchalance completely nonplussed them, and, occupied with their drill, they were effectively diverted from mischief.

Much to the relief of the castle's inmates, the two emissaries returned the same evening from Castlebar. They brought a letter to the bishop from General Trench, giving full assurances regarding the treatment of the rebel prisoners. This was read to the insurgents and appeared to reassure them. More consoling to the bishop was the information, privately imparted by Dean Thompson, that owing to the situation in Killala, the general had decided to commence his march two days earlier than he had intended, and would probably reach them on Sunday morning, the 29th.

The British preparations to suppress the insurrection in northwest Connacht had been considerably delayed by the general unrest in the midlands. There, as mentioned earlier, a widespread rebellion had broken out at the beginning of September; the intention of the rebels being to cooperate with Humbert's army on its march to Dublin. The surrender of Ballinamuck upset their plans, and none of the projected raids took place; but Lord Cornwallis considered it prudent not to remove any troops from the area until he was satisfied that all danger from a renewed outbreak was over. That is why ten days elapsed between the battle of Ballinamuck and General Trench's appearance in Castlebar with an army large enough to restore the king's authority over the entire province.

Trench was determined that no loophole of escape should be left to the rebel forces. His plan was to attack them from different sides, leaving them no alternative but to surrender or be driven into the sea. Lord Portarlington, who was stationed at Sligo, was ordered to march to Ballina and form a junction with the main body from Castlebar. At the same time a force of 300

History as It Happened

of the Armagh militia at Foxford, under Major Acheson, and another 300 men at Newport, under Colonel Fraser, were to converge to the same point from their respective stations. Lord Portarlington's troops, being the farthest away, were the first to move.

Almost 1,000 strong with two pieces of field artillery, they started from Sligo on the morning of September 21. They were not confronted until nightfall, when a body of rebels approached them at their halting place, near the village of Grange. One cannon-shot sufficed to disperse the assailants. The British did not get off so easily on the following night. They had scarcely entered the village of Scarmore when they were attacked by a column of pikemen, who had advanced from Ballina under the command of O'Kane and Berrett. A prolonged and obstinate struggle followed, in which the insurgents were at length beaten. Before the commencement of the action, a number of Protestant farmers living in the neighboring hamlet of Carrowcarden had been impressed into service by the pikemen, and in order to ensure their cooperation they were placed in the first line of battle. The natural consequence of this was their absolute annihilation by the royal troops.

"Extract of a letter from Sligo September 24th.
"The army on their March to Ballina against the rebels, had a severe skirmish with a party of them they came upon up on the road, several of whom they killed and took from them two

> *pieces of cannon. We have just received intelligence here of the annihilation given to the insurgents at Ballina.*
>
> *Our army surrounded them from Scurmore to Ballina and from that to Killala. There were 3,000 of them laid dead in the attack.*
>
> *The King cutter of 14 guns, full of armed men, went from this place to prevent any escape of the insurgents by sea, which had the desired effect. In the march of the army thy burnt all houses where pikes were found, or property plundered from loyal subjects. Among our forces there were two men killed."*

Belfast Newsletter October 6th.

The three remaining British divisions began their march on Saturday, September 22. Major Acheson was vigorously attacked by a rebel detachment but succeeded in beating them off. General Trench took the road that had been used by Humbert on his advance to Castlebar. His progress was slow, for the rain, falling continually, had turned the roadways into beds of mud. The division entered Crossmolina on Saturday night, worn out with the strenuous march. News of their approach reached Killala in the afternoon, and the pikemen at once demanded to be led against the enemy; for with all their drunkenness and disorder, these men were never lacking in courage. Ferdy O'Donnell, of Erris, one of their leaders, placed himself at their head, and the march began. At Rappa the commander was taken sick and the rebel army halted; but a reconnoitring party of three mounted men pushed forward as far as the outskirts of Crossmolina.

They met a picket of sixteen cavalry, whom they attacked and put to flight, following the fugitives into the town itself. The weakness of the reconnoitring party was concealed by the darkness, and their appearance caused an alarm, the drums beating to arms and the soldiers rushing wildly through the streets. Having attained the object of the reconnaissance, the riders departed at full gallop to rejoin their comrades, whom they dissuaded from attacking because ammunition was running short.

The march of General Trench's division was resumed at daybreak and in a couple of hours it entered Ballina to find the town already occupied by Lord Portarlington. Truc and O'Kane had fled at the latter's approach, with the remnant of their followers. In order to seal off all the avenues from Killala, Trench divided his forces, and while advancing with one division by the common highway, he sent the Kerry regiment of militia and some cavalry, under the orders of Lieutenant-Colonel Crosby and Maurice Fitzgerald (commonly known as the Knight of Kerry), to the same destination by a detour through the village of Rappagh.

"Extract of a letter from Ballina, Sept. 2.
We have been for some time here in the
greatest dread of being destroyed by the rebels,

but now, thank God, we have been extricated from those fears-some wretches.

A sore defeat has been given to those deluded wretches by His Majesty's army, in which 1,000 of them were killed between this place and Foxford.

In this vicinity, they caused great depredation. Upon entering the house, they drank any wine they could get, then destroyed the furniture and even the gardens and afterwards carried off all plunder that was portable, to Killala. They were going to hang Colonel Joyce, whose house they plundered.

Some of the French who lately landed at Killala were found among them and are now prisoners."

Belfast Newsletter October 6th.

Bishop Stock thus describes the engagement that followed:

"The peaceful inhabitants of Killala were now to be spectators of a scene they had never expected to behold... a battle; a sight which no person that has seen it once and possesses the feelings of a human creature would choose to witness a second time, A troop of fugitives from Ballina, women and children tumbling over one another to get into the castle, or into any house in the town where they might hope for a

History as It Happened

momentary shelter, continued, for a painful length of time, to give notice of the approach of an army. The rebels quit their camp to occupy the rising ground close by the town; on the road to Ballina, posting themselves under the low stone walls on each side in such a manner as enabled them, with great advantage, to take aim at the king's troops, The two divisions of the royal army were supposed to make up about 1,200 men, and they had five pieces of cannon. The number of the rebels could not be ascertained. Many ran away before the engagement, while a very considerable number flocked into the town in the very heat of it, passing under the castle windows, in view of the French officers on horseback, and running upon death with as little appearance of reflection or concern as if they were hastening to a show. About 400 of these misguided men fell in the battle and immediately after it; whence it may be conjectured that their entire number scarcely exceeded 800 or 900. We kept our eyes on the rebels. They levelled their pieces, fired very deliberately from each side on the advancing enemy: yet (strange to tell) were able only to kill one man, a corporal, and wound one common soldier. Their shot, in general, went over the heads of their opponents, A regiment of Highlanders (Fraser's Fencibles) filed off to the

> *right and left to flank the fusiliers behind the hedges and walls; they had marshy ground on the left to surmount before they could come upon their object, which occasioned some delay, but at length they reached them and made sad havoc among them.*
>
> *"In spite of the exertions of the general and his officers, the town exhibited almost all the marks of a place taken by storm. Some houses were perforated like a riddle; most of them had their doors and windows destroyed, the trembling inhabitants scarcely escaping with life by lying prostrate on the floor. Nor was it till the close of the next day that our ears were relieved from the horrid sound of muskets discharged every minute at flying and powerless rebels."*

In response to Bishop Stock's appeal on his behalf, he was acquitted of the charge, but ordered to leave the country on the shortest notice.

'Two days after the battle the three French officers were ordered to Dublin and one can readily believe the bishop's assertion that he parted with them "not without tears." The story of their honourable and courageous attitude during the long period of disorders having preceded them to the capital, they were received there with many marks of consideration, and they enjoyed the hospitality of no less a person than the lord primate himself

On the report of Bishop Stock, the British Government offered to return them to the French authorities without exchange, but this act of courtey was not accepted by Niou, the French commissary. These men, he declared, had merely followed their line of duty. They had done no more than what was expected of any French officer in a like situation. They were therefore not entitled to special favours.

Appendices

12 Humbert's Subsequent Career

The general and his men were repatriated to France in exchange for British prisoners of war. Here, he resumed his military career.

After a stint in the Army of the Danube, he was sent on an unsuccessful expedition to Saint-Domingue (modern Haiti) 1801 under General Victoire Leclerc to put down a slave revolt. On the voyage across the Atlantic, Humbert was rumoured to have had an affair with Leclerc's wife, who was none other than Napoleon's sister, Pauline Bonaparte.

Naturally enough, Leclerc was not pleased with Humbert, to put it mildly. He ordered him back to France in September 1802.

Napoleon was enraged when he heard of Humber's alleged liaison with his sister and Humbert was stripped of his rank and dismissed from the army.

The reason given was:

"...... for embezzling army rations and selling them for profit, and for having illicit relations with the leaders of the brigands. "

Humbert retired to a château in Brittany, which he had purchased two years earlier.

There he turned to farming and horse dealing. After six years of enforced exile from Paris, he was allowed back into the army for a brief period before he was discharged from active service with a pension of 3,000 francs a year.

In 1812, he emigrated to America where he settled in Philadelphia for several years. However, his restless nature and desire for adventure meant that he couldn't settle there for long.

By 1813, he was in New Orleans, where he busied himself recruiting for an army to invade Texas, (then part of Mexico.)

A number of his colleagues created a "Provisional Government of the Free Men of the Interior Provinces of Mexico. Humbert was given a general's commission and command of the so-called Republican Army of the North.

Unfortunately for the republicans, the president-to-be suddenly switched side and deserted to the royalist (Spanish) side.

Short of funds, Humbert had to return to New Orleans. Here, he began to recruit men for another invasion of Texas, but this came to nothing.

War between England and America broke out in 1812 and wasn't officially ended until the Treaty of Ghent was ratified on Christmas Eve, 1814.

However, news of the treaty didn't reach the combatants for some weeks and in the meantime, the British forces in the Gulf of Mexico launched a major attack on New Orleans.

Given his hatred of all things English, Humbert lost no time in volunteering to fight with the Americans against the invaders. He was given a volunteer commission by the American commander, Andrew Jackson and distinguished himself in the fighting, earning the following acknowledgement from Jackson:

"Gen. Humbert, who offered his services as a volunteer, has constantly exposed himself to the greatest dangers with his characteristic bravery."

The story goes that Jackson and his staff were inspecting the British position through a telescope, ten days after the battle. When Humbert was handed the spyglass and asked his opinion, he looked at the British camp and said, "They're gone!" "How do you know?" asked Jackson. Humbert pointed to a crow that was not afraid to fly close to one of the supposed sentinels, showing it was only a stuffed uniform.

In later years Humbert travelled to Texas and Mexico to take part in adventures there, and upon his return to New Orleans he was arrested for alleged piracy against the Spanish. A group of Frenchmen in Louisiana came to his defence as did the Governor of Louisiana, and he was released.

Thereafter, he lived quietly in a poor district of New Orleans where he supplemented his French army pension by teaching and giving fencing lessons.

A visitor to New Orleans in April 1817 noted:

> *"A gentleman of a certain age, with a powerful voice, sparkling eye and brisk action, sitting in front of me at table. I enquired his name and found that it was General Humbert, the terror of the Spaniards. It was this person who, in the expedition of General Hoche to Ireland, disembarked alone, at the head of the*

> *party he commanded; Unfortunately, he had not received a brilliant education, for which it is so difficult to find a substitute. Although advanced in years he abounds with sense, originality of idea, and an ardor for the cause which he has espoused, while his reputation for personal courage is beyond everything that can be imagined.*
>
> *The collection of this stipend doled out to him every quarter by the French Consul...afforded him the occasion for a great official ceremony. Attired in his old costume of a General of the Republic, the same, perhaps, which he had worn on the heights of Landau or at Castlebar, with his faithful sabre resting across his arm, he would repair, erect and proud, to the consular office on Royal street to receive the pittance allowed by Bonaparte, as the price of his blood on the fields of Europe. Thence, he would gravely walk down the pavement towards his friend...and, after partaking of a glass or two of his unique 'petit gouave,' he would return to his humble lodgings and doff his military trappings."*

Jean Joseph Amable Humbert died in New Orleans on January 3, 1823 at the age of 55. A death notice observed:

"For the last five years his mind had been disordered and a deep melancholy preyed upon his spirits, the consequence of a poverty which left not sufficient to pay the expenses of his funeral."

The Louisiana Courier paid its respects as follows:

> "General Humbert is dead. Born for battles, war was his moment. Taken away, against his will, from that glorious career, if he committed any errors, he nevertheless always remained faithful to honor. A Frenchman and a soldier, he did religiously keep it in his heart, even among the aberrations of an ardent mind still exalted by the misfortunes of his private situation ...
> In combating among us on a soil which formerly was French and against the enemies of France, he thought he had served that country which he adored. Having witnessed his gallantry and his untainted probity, let us throw a veil on the occasional errors of his life and let us deposit some sprigs of laurel on the monument of a brave man, who died far from the theatre of his early glory, but near the spot where his courage shone for the last time."

On January 8, 2015, 200 years after the Battle of New Orleans, a plaque in General Humbert's honour was officially unveiled at New Orleans' St. Louis Cemetery.

13 Jean Sarrazin

Jean Sarrazin, Humbert's most senior subordinate, had a career almost as colourful and varied as his superior's. Before coming to Ireland with Humbert, rumours were circulating that he was a British spy. Obviously, the Directory did not take those allegations seriously, or at least didn't consider his trustworthiness was at issue.

But he was first to surrender at Ballinamuck and did so without Humbert's knowledge or consent. Probably he took the only practical course open to him and saved his own life and those of the men who surrendered with him, but Humbert elected to fight on and was nearly killed in the process.

After the capitulation, the French officers were brought to Dublin and lodged at Corbett's hotel in Capel Street and here Sarrazin was allowed considerably greater freedom of movement than any other of his colleagues.

It was noticeable that, while the Directory did not believe that he was disloyal, his promotions gained under Humbert were not recognised by the government and were only restored to him over a year later years later when the Directory confirmed his promotion to général de brigade and appointed him commander at Angers.

In 1805, when war broke out again, he served as a brigade commander in the VII Corps. His career prospects continued to improve as by 1807 he was the military commander in charge of the département of Lys and then a year later he was given the same position in Escaut in Belgium.

However, here he got into trouble due to disagreements with his superior, General Chambarlhac and he was shunted to the Isle of Cadzand off the coast of Holland. Sarrazin continued with his military career until one day whilst he was employed as an officer at Bologna, he decided that he could stand the French army no longer and simply deserted and fled to England in a fishing boat.

There was much speculation that he was acting as a spy for the English, although nothing was actually proven at the time; however, he was regarded as being a traitor to France. We know from the Alien Register that he arrived in England in June 1810 and that he provided the English with information about Napoleon's army.

He wasted no time when arriving in England and promptly began to complain about the accommodation that the government had provided for him, saying that he would have expected to have stayed in a hotel as he had done in the past; he described his lodgings as like being in prison.

He proved a somewhat prolific letter writer and in 1811 he wrote to a senior minister complaining that he felt he had been badly treated and neglected by the British government and that he had given value and received no equal value in return. He stated that he had delivered notes and plans for the government i.e. he was acting as a spy for them and claimed that he was owed over sixty-two thousand pounds.

At the time of writing this he claimed that he only received £600 and that he was extremely unhappy.

He also stated that his marriage to his first wife in 1799 had been dissolved, however in an account of his claims to the British government for money he wished for it to be recorded that his wife and son were prisoners of war in France. In 1813 he married again, this time to the daughter of a captain in the British army whom he believed was extremely rich. His new wife was only 21 years old and less than half his age.

The marriage was a disaster waiting to happen and after only a couple of months they separated. The couple obviously found a way of putting their differences aside and were reunited a short time later. In 1814, he became a father again when his wife gave birth to a daughter. Sarrazin had left to return to France before his daughter was born, offering his services to Napoleon's military in spite of his desertion in 1810 but, given the manner of his departure they were not interested.

It soon came to light that Sarrazin was not actually free to have married in London and that his first wife Cecilia was still alive. There is no record of what happened to him over the next few years but in May 1817 he married for the third time. This time he married the daughter of his neighbour and he was later to refer to her in very uncomplimentary terms, 'Miss Delard was ugly, lame and raised as a peasant'!

However, his chequered past caught up with him.

The Times of Monday, November 23, 1818 wrote that:

"The noted General Sarrazin, we are informed by our Parisian correspondent; it is currently rumoured, had been committed to prison, on a charge of having married and deserted three wives. One of the unfortunate ladies, it is added, is a branch of a noble Irish family. She has arrived in Paris to prosecute and the French government, very much to its honour conducts the prosecution entirely at its own expense."

The Court of Assizes in Paris tried him for trigamy and found him guilty of this charge and initially sentenced him to the galleys for ten years, to the pillory as well and to pay his second wife, Georgiana Maria, 40 million francs compensation. He was released from prison after three years. After this he was reputed to be leading a sad and transient life in Holland, England, Turkey and Germany.

He died on November 23, 1848, aged 78, and was buried somewhere in Brussels.

14 The Protestant Wind

The British government took part in a coalition of European countries against the new French republic and its ideals. It also provided financial support for the French royalist rebels in the Vendee department (province. The British interference its internal affairs incensed the French Directory and made the already strained relationship between the two countries a good deal worse.

Lazare Hoche, one of France's most popular and successful generals happened to be on friendly terms with Wolfe Tone and other United Irishmen who had come to Paris to lobby the French government for assistance in their attempt to rid Ireland of British rule. Hoche listened to Tone's request for help and was easily persuaded that if the French landed a force in Ireland, thousands of committed Irishmen would rush to join them and a sister republic to the French one could be established.

Hoche used his influence with the Directory to get their support for an expedition to Ireland and he set about organising an invasion force. It was very unfortunate for Hoche and his Irish allies that the expedition was to be launched from Brest where the admiral in charge of naval affairs did not believe that such an expedition could succeed and for months he managed to disrupt and delay Hoche's preparations.

It meant that when Hoche's repeated complaints to the Directory were finally listened to and the naval commander was finally replaced with one who shared Hoche's sentiments, the enterprise, originally scheduled for months earlier was not ready to depart until mid-December 1796.

On December 15, an army of over 15,000 experienced French troops with a vast arsenal of military equipment set sail from Brest. There were 43 warships in total and it was hoped that by sailing in mid-winter they would avoid the English fleet. But the expedition was doomed from the outset.

As the fleet left harbour, bound for Bantry Bay, one of the vessels struck a rock and 1,255 men lost their lives. Only 45 survived.

Then soon after this, Fraternité, with General Hoche onboard, became detached from the flotilla and was unable to rejoin the fleet again.

General Grouchy, his second in command, was unsure if he should land the troops without his commander's presence. While the fleet waited in Bantry Bay, its commanders took no action, Admiral Bouvet grew anxious due to the weather and the possibility of encountering the British navy, but he finally decided to attempt a landing on Christmas Day.

This was a mistake for the weather, which was already stormy, grew much worse and on the 26th, the French were forced to cut ropes and return back to France. 'We were close enough to toss a ship's biscuit ashore," Tone wrote in his diary.

A few days later, the flagship, carrying General Hoche which had been driven westward by the storm and then chased by a British cruiser, arrived at Bantry Bay. And, after speaking with an Irish fisherman, Hoche learned that the French fleet had arrived, waited a few days, and then departed for France. Furious, Hoche returned to France, determined to try again but he died the following year, without getting another chance to land in Ireland.

The Protestant Wind had blown again!

In later years many Irish people firmly believed that God, for some unknown reason, had decided to favour the Protestant population in some way by creating adverse weather conditions whenever a foreign power attempted to invade the country on behalf of the Catholic majority. It is fair to say that a great many Protestants felt the same way.

In 1588, 208 years earlier, Spain attempted to invade England and sent an armada of over 130 ships to accomplish this.

However, the project was hampered by hard luck from beginning to end and most of the ships as well as thousands of its soldiers and sailors never returned home. Totally unexpected unseasonal was the main culprit in this case as the armada set out in late May when the weather could be expected to suit their objectives. Instead, the fleet sailed into an extremely violent gale and a great number of ships either sank or were smashed on the rocky coasts they encountered as they attempted to sail around Scotland and Ireland elude the English navy.

History as It Happened

To stretch coincidence even further, it was well-known that during the Glorious Revolution of 1688, when William of Orange deposed his father-in-law, James 11 as King of England, the invasion fleet bringing William's army from Holland was greatly helped by a change of wind direction as they passed twice in sight of the English fleet, which was unable to intercept because of the adverse wind and an unfavourable tide.

Now, to the superstitious Irish, the fact that the French armada had been shipwrecked couldn't be ascribed to mere coincidence alone.

There was little doubt that God had again interfered in their affairs and not in a positive way.

But Tone and his fellow United men kept on lobbying Directory ministers and in a surprisingly short time, another invasion of Ireland was arranged.

This time however, the French were not directly involved. This proposed invasion was organised and manned by Batavia, the modern state of Holland, at the insistence of the sister republic.

Coupled with the loss in men and resources as a result of the failed Bantry Bay expedition, the French were stretched the limit by the demands put on its resources by Napoleon Bonaparte as he prepared for an invasion of Egypt. Tone and his comrades were bitterly disappointed when the found out that Bonaparte had shelved any plans he may have had to assist the Irish rebels and was now looking eastwards to Egypt instead.

The Dutch managed to assemble a formidable force and got ready to put to sea in early June 1797.

The Last Invasion of Ireland

But pure bad luck, or the proverbial Protestant wind, upset their plans. On the point of departure, the wind changed direction and began to blow onshore, thereby preventing the Dutch setting sail. After failing to sail out of port for a number of days, the troops were disembarked and the plans for the expedition were abandoned. The window of opportunity had closed firmly once again.

Unknown to the Dutch, the Royal Navy would probably have been unable to prevent their crossing to Ireland if the winds had been more favourable. Two of the naval ports were crippled by mutiny and Sir Adam Duncan, in charge of the British fleet monitoring the Dutch preparations was unable to dock at the Nore and Shiphead shipyards to restock and to have repairs carried out.

In October, the Dutch commander was ordered to proceed to Brest to link up with a French force being assembled there in preparation for another invasion of Ireland. The Dutch fleet was intercepted by Duncan and in a major naval battle, the Royal Navy destroyed or captured the majority of the Dutch fleet.

Bad luck continued to dog the French once more as preparations for another invasion force went ahead. This time, the invaders were to be split into three separate armies.

One, under General Hardy was to sail from Brest and the second one was commanded by General Humbert, based in La Rochelle. The third and the largest one was to have been commanded by an Irishman, Charles Edward Jennings, better known as Kilmaine. Hardy's force of 3,000 men was scheduled to set out first and he was to be closely followed by Humbert with his smaller force.

Kilmaine was to be held back until the other two generals had landed and, if the prospects of success were encouraging, he was scheduled to follow with his force of over 11,000 soldiers. Unfortunately, for the success of the French and Irish prospects, Humbert did not follow the plan.

He decided to sail before he had completed provisioning and it seems he wanted to get to Ireland before Hardy as he knew that Hardy would assume control of both armies when they had each landed. This he wanted to avoid at all costs, and he took a major gamble by embarking before Hardy was aware of what he intended to do. He believed the substance of what Wolfe Tone; Napper Tandy and his own aide-de-camp had told him. So, he expected to find thousands of volunteers who would be ready, willing and able to provide him with the manpower that was crucial to his initiative's success.

He wasn't to know as his invasion fleet put to sea that the rebels in Wexford had risen up in rebellion in May and had been crushed mercilessly. There had been outbreaks in both Down and Antrim during the month of June, but both had been crushed.

Admiral Savary who commanded Humbert's ships decided to sail well out into the Atlantic to lessen the chances of being spotted by the Royal Navy who were patrolling the seas off the coast of Ireland, anticipating a French assault. Savary managed to bring all three ships safely to anchor in Killala Bay, which was a remarkable feat of sailing, but the French forces were hungry, seasick and in general poor fighting shape when they landed.

They had been at sea for over three weeks and had run into a succession of North Atlantic gales on the way.

Bearing that in mind, it's astonishing that they were able to achieve so much in such a short period of time when they routed the English army at Castlebar and took possession of the town less than five days after landing at Kilcummin over 60 km away to the north.

By the time Hardy set sail, on September 16, Humbert had already been defeated at Ballinamuck and the possibilities of an Irish uprising anywhere on the island were remote.

Having missed one invasion force, the Royal Navy was on alert for another, and when the squadron carrying Hardy's forces left Brest it was soon spotted. After a long chase, the French were cornered in Lough Swilly, a bay off the County Donegal coast close to Tory Island. During the action the outnumbered French fleet attempted to escape, but were run down and defeated piecemeal, with the British capturing four ships and scattering the survivors. Over the next fortnight, British frigate patrols scoured the passage back to Brest, capturing three more ships. Of the ten ships in the original French squadron, only two frigates and a schooner reached safety. British losses in the campaign were minimal.

The battle marked the last attempt by the French Navy to launch an invasion of any part of the British Isles. It also ended the last hopes the United Irishmen had of obtaining outside support in their struggle with the British. After the action, Tone was recognised aboard the captured French flagship and arrested.

Apparently, he believed that, due to his rank in the French army, he would be classed as a prisoner of war and would eventually be repatriated along with his fellow officers. He had been given the opportunity to escape on a lighter ship when it became obvious that the flagship, on which he commanded a gun battery, was too slow to flee.

He spurned the offer to transfer to another ship and fought to the very end. Onlookers said he was most indignant when he was shackled as a "common rebel" and protested at the indignity inflicted on an officer on the army of the republic.

A copy of his letter of protest to Lord Cavan, the British commanding officer in the region is included in the next chapter. Cavan's reply is included also, and it is very obvious that he had little sympathy with Tone's claims.

15 Theobald Wolfe Tone

Wolfe Tone may not have sailed with Humbert, but he still played a central part in the proceedings. He, more than anyone else, persuaded the French Directory to aid the United Irishmen in their struggle for independence.

Tone was an adjutant general in the French army and was one of General Hardy's forces preparing to sail from Brest when Humbert ignored the Directory's orders and departed first.

Unlike Humbert, Hardy was intercepted by an English fleet and after a fierce naval battle off the coast of Donegal, the French were defeated and many, including Hardy and Wolfe Tone, were captured.

Some of the lighter, faster French ships escaped but the command ship, the Hoche, was forced to surrender and those onboard were imprisoned. Tone had been given the opportunity to depart on one of the ships that escaped but he refused to do so and was recognised by some of his captors.

It is not clear why he did not depart when advised to flee by his colleagues, but it may have been because he thought his status as a French officer would ensure that he would be regarded as a prisoner of war.

According to contemporary reports, he was very indignant and felt insulted when he was segregated from his fellow officers and put in chains. He wrote a strong letter of protest to Lord Cavan, the army officer commanding the North Donegal area, but Cavan's reply was uncompromising. (Tone had used the pseudonym, Smith, when he was captured.)

"Derry prison, 12 Brumaire, 6th year-
"My Lord, Nov. 3. 1798.
On my arrival here, Major Chester informed me that on the orders of your Lordship. In consequence, as I presume, of the directions of Government, were that I should be put in irons; I take it for granted; those orders were issued in ignorance of the rank I have the honour to hold in the armies of the French Republic.
I am, in consequence, to apprize your Lordship, that I am breveted as Chef de Brigade in the Infantry, since the 1st Merflidor, an. 4; that I have been promoted to the rank of Adjutant-General the 2d. Nivose, an. 6; and, finally, that I have served as such, attached to General Hardy since the 3d. Thermidor, an. 6, by virtue of the orders of the Minister at War.

Major Chester, to whom I have shown my commissions, can satisfy your Lordship as to the fact and General Hardy will ascertain the authenticity of the documents. Under these circumstances, I address myself to your Lordship as a man of honour and a soldier; and I do protest in the most precise and strongest manner against the indignity intended against the honour of the French Army in my person; and I claim the rights and privileges of a prisoner of war- agreeable to my rank and situation in an army, not less to be respected in all points than any other which exists in Europe.

From the situation your Lordship holds under your Government, I must presume you have a discretionary power to act according to circumstances; I cannot for a moment doubt that what I have now explained to your Lordship will induce you to give immediate orders that the honour of the French Nation and the French Army be respected in my person; and that of course I shall suffer no coercion other than in common with the rest of my brave comrades, whom the fortune of war has for the moment deprived of their liberty.
"I am, my Lord, with great respect,
"Your Lordship's most obedient servant,
"T.W. Tone, dit Smith, Adj. Gen."

ANSWER
FROM MAJOR-GENERAL THE EARL OF CAVAN TO THEOBALD WOLFE TONE.
Rarnacranna, Nov. 3, 1798.
"Sir,

"I have received your letter of this date from Derry Gaol, in which you inform me that you consider being ordered into irons as an insult and degradation of the rank you hold in the army of the French Republic, and that you protest in the most precise and strongest manner against such indignity. Had you been a native of France, or any other country not belonging to the British empire, indisputably it would be so; but the motive that directed me to give the order I did this morning for you being put in irons was, that I looked on you (and you have proved yourself) a traitor and rebel to your Sovereign and native country, and as such you shall be treated by me.

"I shall enforce the order I gave this morning; and I can lament a man the fate that awaits you: - every indulgence shall be granted you by me individually, that is not inconsistent with my public duty.
"I am, Sir, your humble servant,
"CAVAN, Major-Gen."

The Last Invasion of Ireland

Tone was court martialled and sentenced to death. He accepted his guilt and said he was prepared to die but he wished to be shot like a soldier. His request was refused.
The Staffordshire Advertiser (17th Nov 1798) carried this report on those proceedings.

"TONE

Dublin Nov. 10th. This day, T. W. Tone was capitally convicted by a court-martial at the barracks, of which General Loftus was President. Tone being asked on his trial whether he was guilty or not of the charge of having as a false traitor entered into the service of the enemy, and appeared in arms against his Sovereign? He replied that he would give the court no trouble; that he fully admitted the charge. He then read a defense, in doing which he was at three different inflammatory passages stopped by the Court and ordered to erase the obnoxious parts out of the paper.
The general tendency of this paper was that he confessed having entered the French service (and he produced his commission as Chef de Brigade) that he had embarked on the great design of raising three millions of his fellow-subjects from a state of bondage; that he had made the same attempt in

which Washington had succeeded, and Kosciusko had failed; to the Catholicks of Ireland he acknowledged his obligations, he had engaged sincerely in their service, and had been amply remunerated; the connexion of Ireland with Great-Britain he had ever considered as bane and he had acted under this conviction to rescue his country; success he could not command, and he was prepared to meet his fate.

As a soldier, however, he wished to die as a soldier; he wished as an emigrant taken in arms to be treated as the French had treated the Count de Sombreuil, and to be shot; the sooner his fate was to take place, the better; he wished it might be within an hour.

Since the trial of Mr. Tone, he begged that no one would be admitted to see him, not even his closest relations. He lay in bed on Sunday, until the middle of the day. Early on Monday morning, he cut his throat, but not so effectually as he wished to terminate his life. A razor was the instrument he used in this desperate effort, as he lay in bed, attended by guards. It was intended to execute him yesterday at the front of the new Prison, but the following occurrence prevented that event.

Yesterday, application was made by Counsellors Curran and Johnson to the Court of King's Bench, for an Habeas Corpus to bring before the court Theobald Wolfe Tone, grounded on an affidavit of his father, Mr. Peter Tone, purporting that Theob. Wolfe Tone was tried by a Court Martial, on a charge of High Treason, and was ordered for execution, though the said T. Wolfe Tone did not belong to his Majesty's army, &c. And that such proceedings and sentence was pronounced during the sitting of his Majesty's law courts.
The Court ordered the Habeas Corpus, and that the prisoner should be brought up to the bar of the Court instanter.

In some short time, an answer was made to the Court, that Theobald Wolfe Tone was unfit to be brought up, having dangerously wounded himself, and the surgeon belonging to the 5th. Dragoons appeared to give testimony, the Court ordered him to be examined, when he deposed that he had visited T.W. Tone in the Provost Marshalsea, who was incapable of being removed in consequence of his making an attempt on his life, having with a razor cut his throat across nearly from ear to ear, and also separated the wind-pipe- that languishing

> *under his present condition, he could not be lifted without immediate danger to his life. The business remained so far undetermined, as not to adit of any further proceedings until the recovery of the prisoner."*
>
> Staffordshire Advertiser ...17th Nov 1798

Tone's father, Peter, engaged the services of a prominent barrister, John Philpott Curran, to defend his son. Curran applied to the King's Bench to issue a habeas corpus writ to force the military authorities to release Wolfe Tone from custody so his case could be heard by a civilian court. The probability seems to be that his hopes of escaping the death penalty would be better if this happened.

Incidentally, Curran was the father of Sarah, Robert Emmet's sweetheart.

After he was found guilty, Tone was given the opportunity to enter a reply in his defence. The following exchange is reproduced courtesy of the United Irishman website. It would appear from the available evidence that Wolfe Tonne committed suicide but there was a strong suspicion that he may have been murdered.

> *"The members of the Court having been sworn, the Judge Advocate called on the prisoner to plead guilty or not guilty to the charge of having acted traitorously and hostilely against the King.*

TONE REPLIED: "I mean not to give the court any useless trouble and wish to spare them the idle task of examining witnesses. I admit all the facts alleged, and only request leave to read an address which I have prepared for this occasion."

COLONEL DALY: "I must warn the prisoner that, in acknowledging those facts, he admits, to his prejudice that he has acted traitorously against his Majesty. Is such his intention?"

TONE: "Stripping this charge of the technicality of its terms, it means, I presume, by the word traitorously, that I have been found in arms against the soldiers of the King in my native country. I admit this accusation in its most extended sense and request again to explain to the court the reasons and motives of my conduct."

The court then observed they would hear his address, provided he kept himself within the bounds of moderation.
Tone rose, and began in these words:

"Mr. President and Gentlemen of the Court-Martial, I mean not to give you the trouble of bringing judicial proof to convict me legally of

having acted in hostility to the government of his Britannic Majesty in Ireland. I admit the fact. From my earliest youth I have regarded the connection between Great Britain and Ireland as the curse of the Irish nation, and felt convinced that, whilst it lasted, this country could never be free nor happy. My mind has been confirmed in this opinion by the experience of every succeeding year, and the conclusions which I have drawn from every fact before my eyes. In consequence,

I was determined to employ all the powers which my individual efforts could move, in order to separate the two countries. That Ireland was not able of herself to throw off the yoke, I knew; I therefore sought for aid wherever it was to be found. In honourable poverty I rejected offers which, to a man in my circumstances, might be considered highly advantageous. I remained faithful to what I thought the cause of my country, and sought in the French Republic an ally to rescue three million of my countrymen from—"

The President here interrupted the prisoner, observing that this language was neither relevant to the charge, nor such as ought to be delivered in a public court.

A Member said it seemed calculated only to inflame the minds of a certain description of people (the United Irishmen), many of whom might be present, and that the court could not suffer it.

THE JUDGE ADVOCATE SAID: "If Mr. Tone meant this paper to be laid before his Excellency in way of extenuation, it must have quite a contrary effect, if the foregoing part was suffered to remain."

The President wound up by calling on the prisoner to hesitate before proceeding further in the same strain.

TONE THEN CONTINUED: "I believe there is nothing in what remains for me to say which can give any offence; I mean to express my feelings and gratitude towards the Catholic body, in whose cause I was engaged."

PRESIDENT: "That seems to have nothing to say to the charge against you, to which you are only to speak. If you have anything to offer in defence or extenuation of the charge, the court will hear you, but they beg you will confine yourself to that subject."

TONE: "I shall, then, confine myself to some points relative to my connection with the

French army. Attached to no party in the French Republic—without interest, without money, without intrigue—the openness and integrity of my views raised me to a high and confidential rank in its armies. I obtained the confidence of the Executive Directory, the approbation of my generals, and I will venture to add, the esteem and affection of my brave comrades.

When I review these circumstances, I feel a secret and internal consolation which no reverse of fortune, no sentence in the power of this court to inflict, can deprive me of, or weaken in any degree. Under the flag of the French Republic I originally engaged with a view to save and liberate my own country. For that purpose, I have encountered the chances of war amongst strangers; for that purpose, I repeatedly braved the terrors of the ocean, covered, as I knew it to be, with the triumphant fleets of that power which it was my glory and my duty to oppose. I have sacrificed all my views in life; I have courted poverty; I have left a beloved wife unprotected, and children whom I adored fatherless. After such a sacrifice, in a cause which I have always considered—conscientiously considered—as the cause of justice and freedom, it is no great effort, at this day, to add the sacrifice of my life. But I hear it said that this unfortunate country has been a prey to all sorts of horrors. I sincerely lament it. I beg; however, it may be remembered that I have been absent four years from Ireland. To me these sufferings can never be attributed. I designed by fair and open war to procure the separation of the two countries. For open war I was prepared, but instead of that a system of private assassination has taken place. I repeat, whilst I deplore it, that it is not chargeable on me. Atrocities, it seems, have been committed on both sides. I do not less deplore them. I detest them from my heart; and to those who know my character and sentiments I may safely appeal for the truth of this assertion; with them I need no justification.

In a case like this success is everything. Success, in the eyes of the vulgar, fixes its merits. Washington succeeded, and Kosciusko failed. After a combat nobly sustained—combat which would have excited the respect and sympathy of a generous enemy—my fate has been to become a prisoner, to the eternal disgrace of those who gave the orders. I was brought here in irons like a felon. I mention this for the sake of others; for me, I am indifferent to it. I am aware of the fate which awaits me, and scorn equally the tone of complaint and that of supplication. As to the connection between this country and Great

Britain, I repeat it—all that has been imputed to me (words, writings, and actions), I here deliberately avow. I have spoken and acted with reflection and on principle and am ready to meet the consequences. Whatever be the sentence of the court, I am prepared for it. Its members will surely discharge their duty—I shall take care not to be wanting in mine."

The court having asked if he wished to make any further observation,
TONE: *"I wish to offer a few words relative to one single point—the mode of punishment. In France our emigrees, who stand nearly in the same situation in which I now stand before you, are condemned to be shot. I ask that the court shall adjudge me the death of a soldier and let me be shot by a platoon of grenadiers. I request this indulgence rather in consideration of the uniform I wear—the uniform of a Chef de Brigade in the French army—than from any personal regard to myself. In order to evince my claim to this favour, I beg that the court may take the trouble to peruse my commission and letters of service in the French army. It will appear from these papers that I have not received them as a mask to cover me, but that I have been long and bona fide an officer in the French service."*

JUDGE ADVOCATE: "You must feel that the papers you allude to will serve as undeniable proof against you."

TONE: "Oh, I know they will. I have already admitted the facts, and I now admit the papers as full proof of conviction."

[The papers were then examined; they consisted of a brevet of Chef de Brigade from the Directory, signed by the Minister of War, of a letter of service granting to him the rank of Adjutant-General, and of a passport.]

GENERAL LOFTUS: "In these papers you are designated as serving in the army of England."

TONE: "I did serve in that army, when it was commanded by Buonaparte, by Dessaix, and by Kilmaine, who is, as I am, an Irishman; but I have also served elsewhere."

The Court requested if he had anything further to observe.

He said that nothing more occurred to him, except that the sooner his Excellency's approbation of the sentence was obtained the better.

(For a long time, a section of the speech was suppressed, the court having forbade it's reading at the trial. It was not until the publication of the "Correspondence" of Lord Cornwallis (Lord Lieutenant in Ireland at the time) decades later that the suppressed passage came to light, in which he thanks the Catholics of Ireland. I have included it below)
"I have laboured to abolish the infernal spirit of religious persecution, by uniting the Catholics and Dissenters. To the former I owe more than ever can be repaid. The service I was so fortunate as to render them they rewarded munificently; but they did more: when the public cry was raised against me—when the friends of my youth swarmed off and left me alone—the Catholics did not desert me; they had the virtue even to sacrifice their own interests to a rigid principle of honour; they refused, though strongly urged, to disgrace a man who, whatever his conduct towards the Government might have been, had faithfully and conscientiously discharged his duty towards them; and in so doing, though it was in my own case, I will say they showed an instance of public virtue of which I know not whether there exists another example."

16 The Trial and Conviction of Mr. Bart. Teeling

Teeling was brought to Dublin and put on trial for his life. He was court martialled and found guilty and was subsequently hanged.

"The trial and conviction of Mr. Bart. Teeling"
Dublin, Sept. 20. This day, the Court Martial, met for the trial of Mr. Bartholomew Teeling, sat at the barracks. The following are the minutes of its proceedings:
"The Court was composed of the following Officers:
Colonel M'Guinness, President,
Lord Gosford,
Lord Enniskillen,
Colonel Innes,
Lieut. Col. Daly,
Lieut. Col. Farley,
Major Ponsonby.

"On being brought forward for trial, the prisoner presented the Court an affidavit which

he said he was ready to subscribe. It stated the necessity of certain persons resident in Castlebar, to attend as witnesses for him, and also the attendance of the French General Humbert, and therefore requiring the postponement of his trial.

The court was cleared for the purpose of deciding on this request; and on the readmission of visitors, the Judge Advocate declared that the court had not decided positively on the subject; but they conceived it better to go into the evidence for the prosecution; after which, if they should so conclude, they might grant the object of the affidavit. The Court accordingly proceeded. William Coulson was called, for the purpose of identifying the prisoner, and proving him to be a natural born subject of the King; but Mr. Teeling precluded the necessity of such an examination by acknowledging himself to be a native of Ireland; but that on going into the service of France, he had changed his name to that of Veron.

"*Michael Burke was then sworn, He deposed of having gone to Castlebar on the 31st.of August, where he saw the prisoner, who told him he had come with the French; that he saw the prisoner act as a French officer, under the command of the Commander in Chief, Humbert;*

that he told the witness of having fled this country about 14 months ago, assigning for reason that the Government has issued an order for putting him to death. Mr. Teeling observed, on the inactivity of some gentlemen in the neighbourhood, who had notice of the invasion, and who should not be so tardy in joining the French although the Government should burn their houses; adding that his house in the North had been burned by the Army.

The witness further deposed that he had been in Castlebar from Friday until the Tuesday following, during which he saw the prisoner particularly active in causing pikes to be made, for the purpose of arming the rebels who should join the French forces. From Castlebar the witness accompanied the invader to Collooney, where he took occasion to quit them previous to the action which was fought on that place. Being asked what occasioned his going to Castlebar, he replied that he went thither as a spy for the purpose of obtaining information for the Government, and that he had left the French as soon as he could obtain a pass from the persons empowered to grant it.
He said that it was through Mr. Teeling and others, who spoke English, that the French Commander principally issued his orders, and

that they saw them execute, and he concluded his evidence by saying that Mr. Teeling was most exemplary while he was a witness of it.
No other evidence having been adduced in support of the prosecution. The prisoner briefly informed the court again, of the necessity there was for the presence of witnesses from Castlebar and that of General Humbert.
He also stated that his agent would be obliged to go to the assizes of Armagh, and in consideration of all of those circumstances, he prayed the Court for such time as would appear to them necessary for obviating those difficulties which lay in the way of his defence.

The Judge Advocate answered that as to the production of General Humbert, the prisoner might put that out of his head, and as to the other persons, he did not conceive that their presence was material to his defence.
If he wished the letters that were written by General Humbert in his favour be submitted to his Majesty with the minutes of the correspondence, it should be done, and from anything that was apparent, those letters amply supplied the absence of the writer of them. The Judge Advocate deprecated delay; he said the court was formed for the acceleration of the ends of justice, and if the question of the

required witnesses went to the merits of the case, every inclination would be felt to support it but he (the Judge Advocate) felt that no better palliatory evidence could be adduced than that of the witness for the prosecution; for it appeared from the evidence of Burke, that the conduct of the prisoner was such as to challenge the approbation, even of a man who had obtained a knowledge of his conduct, for the purpose of hostile observation.

Mr. Teeling said that the court must have observed that it was not his intention to give any unnecessary delay, and he would, conformably to this disposition, acknowledge that the witnesses from Castlebar were intended merely for a palliative purpose. The court, on this, observed that the evidence in his favour came stronger from the person prosecuting, than if proceeding from a hundred persons brought by himself; but if he wished to say anything defensive in manner of address, the court was ready to hear it.

The prisoner replied, that if it was inconvenient to the court to adjourn to Saturday, he would enter on his defence to-morrow (Friday) but the extended period would suit his interests better; on which the court adjourned until to-morrow and told the prisoner to come up on Saturday to make his defence.

Teeling is a handsome, active, young man, of good address, and about 25 to 30 years of age; he was dressed in the undress fashion of the French officers, wore large rings in his ears, and conversed with much unseeming concern with his friends and relatives, who were around him. He said in reply to the enquiry of some of his friends, "that he was very well used, and wanted for nothing but a little of his Majesty's liberty."

Sept. 23.

At twelve o'clock this morning Teeling was brought into court, pursuant to adjournment from Tuesday. He read his defence, Teeling is a handsome, active, young man, of good address, and about 25 to 30 years of age; he was dressed in the undress fashion of the French officers, wore large rings in his ears, and conversed with much unseeming concern with his friends and relatives, who were around him. He said in reply to the enquiry of some of his friends, "that he was very well used, and wanted for nothing but a little of his Majesty's liberty."

Sept. 23.- At twelve o'clock this morning Teeling was brought into court, pursuant to adjournment from Tuesday. He read his defence, which occupied three folio pages. It commenced injudiciously as many Lawyers have asserted, with implied suspicions of the jurisdiction of the court, emphatically contradicting the disadvantages he might be presumed to labour under, with the superior chances he might have if tried by Civil Law.

The main point of his defence was, however, concise, merely stating that having been bred in France, though a native of Ireland, he entered early into the Republican army, where he attained to some rank, that at the time the last French expedition was projected, he was at La Rochelle, where he received orders from General Humbert to join the destined embarkation with all possible dispatch; that he thought it his duty to comply, as refusal would not only be certain death to him, but stamp his name with infamy. He averted, as extenuating circumstances, to the humanity of his conduct since his arrival in Ireland, as appeared by the testimony of his prosecutor; and concluded with the usual ceremony of reliance on the justice and mercy of the court, and some personal compliments to the Lord Lieutenant.

He was adjudged Death, though not formally, until the sentence is sanctioned by the Lord Lieutenant."

Teeling attempted to read the following statement from the scaffold but was not permitted to.

> "Fellow-citizens, I have been condemned by a military tribunal to suffer what they call an ignominious death, but what appears, from the number of its illustrious victims, to be glorious in the highest degree. It is not in the power of men to abase virtue nor the man who dies for it. His death must be glorious in the field of battle or on the scaffold.
>
> The same Tribunal which has condemned me —Citizens, I do not speak to you here of the constitutional right of such a Tribunal, —has stamped me a traitor. If to have been active in endeavouring to put a stop to the blood-thirsty policy of an oppressive Government has been treason, I am guilty. If to have endeavoured to give my native country a place among the nations of the earth was treason, then I am guilty indeed. If to have been active in endeavouring to remove the fangs of oppression from the head of the devoted Irish peasant was treason, I am guilty.
>
> Finally, if to have striven to make my fellow-men love each other was guilt, then I am guilty.

You, my countrymen, may perhaps one day be able to tell whether these were the acts of a traitor or deserved death. My own heart tells me they were not and, conscious of my innocence, I would not change my present situation for that of the highest of my enemies. Fellow-citizens, I leave you with the heartfelt satisfaction of having kept my oath as a United Irishman, and with the glorious prospect of the success of the cause in which we have been engaged. Persevere, my beloved countrymen. Your cause is the cause of Truth. It must and will ultimately triumph."

Hull Advertiser and Exchange Gazette - Saturday 29 September

"He is believed to have been buried at the mass grave of rebels at Croppies' Acre, Dublin. The fate of the condemned young man called forth immense sympathy in Dublin and throughout the provincial towns, but especially in those parts of Ulster where his name was so much associated with that chivalrous love of country which the native Irish look upon as the noblest of all virtues. Considerable influence was used in the hope of obtaining a remission of the sentence, but the authorities were inexorable, and the imperious Cornwallis refused to meet a deputation of mercy. In vain

were all appeals to the Viceroy, and the plea that the condemned aide-de-camp had been the means of saving the lives of the captive officers at Castlebar made no impression on the chief of Dublin Castle. "The law must take its course," was the reply of the Lord Lieutenant."

Finns Leinster Journal - Saturday 29 September 1798

17 Contemporary Newspaper Quotes

The following clips are verbatim reports from contemporary newspapers of the period. None of there were, or could have been expected to be, fair and impartial reporting.

There were three Irish papers of note in 1798, The Belfast Newsletter, The Freemans Journal and Finns Leinster Journal. The Belfast Newsletter was at this time very anti-Catholic and the other two, while nowhere nearly as sectarian, were expected to follow official policy. This was in part due to government censorship but also it should be kept in mind that the vast majority of newspaper readers at this time were Protestant and Loyalist to the core as well.

Even if somebody felt safe to openly support the French republican cause (and it definitely wasn't) lack of readership would have forced the paper into liquidation.

Extracts from a wide range of English newspapers of the period are included and without exception all toed the official line, which was to be expected. Yet, while they mainly depended on military sources for their information, there seems little sign of anti-Catholic bias in their reporting.

When Humbert left Ballina on his march to Castlebar on 22 August, he left a corps of French officers and soldiers behind,

History as It Happened

about 200 men in all. They were left there to preserve the peace, basically to prevent widespread looting of property and the taking of life. In both cases, the local Protestant minority was most at risk.

The danger of a seaborne attack from Sligo could have cut his lines of communication and resulted in the loss of a considerable amount of gunpowder and other military supplies that were stored in the bishop's palace in Killala.

The French left behind controlled Killala, Ballina and the surrounding district but the French presence in the region was considerably reduced when Humbert sent an urgent order to the commander in charge to send all but three officers, Ponson, Boudet and Truc, to strike out to join up with him as he marched through Sligo county. This they did, by marching through the Windy Gap in the Ox Mountains and meeting the main party near Tubbercurry.

The people most affected when the French moved out, were in great far of their lives as can be seen in this report from the Belfast Newsletter dated September 2 but published on October 6.

"Extract of a letter from Ballina, Sept. 2.
"We have been for some time here in the greatest dread of being destroyed by the rebels, but now, thank God, we have been extricated from those fears-.
A sore defeat has been given to those deluded wretches by His Majesty's army, in which 1,000 of them were killed between this place and

> *Foxford. In this vicinity, they caused great depredation. On entering the house, they drank any wine they could get, then destroyed the furniture and even the gardens and afterwards carried off all plunder that was portable, to Killala. They were going to hang Colonel Joyce, whose house they plundered. Some of the French who lately landed at Killala were found among them and are now prisoners."*
>
> Freeman's Journal, Thursday, September 27, 1798.

Admiral Savary brought Humbert and his soldiers to County Mayo. In order to evade Royal Navy patrols, he sailed far out into the Atlantic until he was in line with the north Mayo coast and he then veered sharply right and sailed directly in. He followed a circuitous route and encountered a series of storms on the way, but his priority was to avoid detection and in this he was successful.

However, this safe journey came at a price. The ships were at sea for over three weeks and the conditions on board must have been cramped and uncomfortable, each ship transported over 450 people and were loaded heavily with military supplies and equipment.

(It should be remembered also that ships such as those commanded by Savary were designed for the transport of personnel and the safety of all aboard was the main concern, whereas as the enemy were geared for search and destroy missions. This is one of the reasons why French attempts to invade Ireland during this period were spectacularly unsuccessful.) Like Humbert and other French officials were accustomed to doing, Savary ensured that his superiors, the French Directory, were kept fully informed about his achievements.

Savary took care to trumpet his own achievements and he just ignored anything that did not suit his interests.

"(Extract of a letter from Citizen Savary, Chief of a Naval Division, written to the Minister of the Marine, in the Road of Royan, at the mouth of the Gironde.")

"I take the earliest opportunity of acquainting you on my return to France, after having landed in the bay of Killala, in Ireland, the troops of the Republic, which you ordered me to convey thither."

"I bring in return some English prisoners, who belonged to the garrison of Killala, which place was carried by some French grenadiers under the orders of General Sarrazin, while the landing of the other troops was completed- Words cannot express the spirit and order displayed by the soldiers during the landing; every soldier was a hero. On the day following, (the 23rd of August) an action took place wherein Gen. Humbert defeated the enemy, who lost 100 men in killed and wounded."

> *"The 24th was to be another glorious day for the French. My gallant comrades, as well as myself, were very much concerned at being obliged to set sail on account of the approaching boisterous weather, else we would have had more prisoners to take with us. On my departure 1,5000 Irish had joined our troops and were organized; 20,000 were waiting for us at a small distance--Long live the Republic."*
> *(Signed) "SAVARY."*
>
> Tuesday, September 25, 1798; (Belfast Newsletter)

Humbert delayed for over a week in Castlebar thereby allowing Cornwallis to assemble a huge army in Athlone and to prevent him crossing the Shannon and gain entry into the midlands. Lake was also preparing to advance against him from the south and the French were in danger of being trapped in a giant pincer movement.

He had gambled heavily by leaving La Rochelle before Hardy had sailed from Brest, contrary to the Directory's directive. He did not know that Hardy would not put to sea until after his own defeat at Ballinamuck or that his invasion was going to end in failure.

Hardy's ships were intercepted at Lough Swilly as he was preparing to disembark in Donegal and after a fierce gunfight, his flagship, The Hoche, was captured. Wolfe Tone has been on board and was taken prisoner.

As Humbert delayed too long in Castlebar, he had no realistic hopes of evading the net that encircled him and his army at Ballinamuck over 180 km. away.

The following extract, taken from Finns Leinster Journal, was based on a briefing from a military source and this is very obvious as the bias in favour of the government's agenda is obvious. At Carricknagat for instance the Franco- Irish troops numbered at most 1,500 men. Colonel Vereker, the English commander had roughly an equal number.

While it may not have suited those, who chose to regard the Irish who joined Humbert as freedom fighters struggling for a United Ireland, the reality is that they contained men of all manners and means in their midst.

It was clear from the outset that the French soldiers had grave reservations about their new Irish allies.

> *"A correspondent mentions that the conduct of the French soldiery, who landed at Killala, to the Rebels and Deserters who joined them, was highly ludicrous and at the same time most wisely cautious.*
> *They affected to meet the Rebels with Republican Fraternity, saying "Erin go Braugh," but when the Erinites would make too free and want to mess with them, the French soldiers, not liking too close an acquaintance with traitors, always desired the Rebels in broken English to keep their own company."*

Thursday, October 25, 1798; (Freemans Journal)

The following brief dispatch sent by Lord Cornwallis to a senior government official. It was written in the wake of the debacle at Ballinamuck and is self-explanatory.

"London Gazette Extraordinary:
WHITEHALL, SEPTEMBER 12.
A dispatch, of which the following is a copy, has been received this morning from his Excellency the Lord Lieutenant of Ireland, by his Grace the Duke of Portland, one of his Majesty's principal Secretaries of State.
St. John's Town, County of Longford, September 8th, 1798.
"My LORD, I have the satisfaction to inform your Grace, that the French troops which landed in this country have surrendered at discretion, after sustaining for some time an attack from the column under General Lake. The Rebels who had joined them were dispersed, and a great proportion of them killed or taken. I cannot at present ascertain the numbers either of the French or Rebels, but I believe that both were inconsiderable.
I have not had an opportunity of seeing General Lake since the action and can therefore at present give your Grace no further

> *particulars, than that no officer was killed or materially wounded."*
> *"I am, &c. Cornwallis."*
> *HIs Grace, the Duke of Portland, &c. &c.*
>
> Oxford Journal - Saturday 15 September 1798

Newspapers in both jurisdictions kept a close eye on proceedings and reported on a daily basis on the movements of both Humbert and his adversaries. The Chester Chronicle carried the following report on the activity in North Leitrim after Humbert had crossed the Shannon and was approaching Cloone on the Longford/Leitrim border.

> *"On Saturday the following Bulletin was issued from Dublin Castle: --*
> *Dublin Castle, Sept. 8.*
> *Advices have been received this evening from head-quarters at Carrick on Shannon, by which it appears that the enemy had passed through Manor Hamilton and crossed the river at Ballintra. They threw away eight guns and two tumbrels in their march, deserting them. General Lake was following them with his corps.- His Excellency was marching on Mohill. A body of Insurgents having collected near Granard on Wednesday last, several Yeoman Corps in the neighbourhood, and from the county of Cavan, commanded by Captain Cottingham, collected with celerity, and entirely*

> *defeated the enemy at the town of Granard, killing about 150, and dispersing the remainder. The Yeomanry experienced no loss. On the same evening, Lord Longford, at the head of a body of yeomanry, assisted by a detachment of the King's troops, attacked a body of Rebels at Wilson's Hospital, and put them to flight with much slaughter."*
>
> Chester Chronicle - Friday 28 September 1798

It soon became obvious that all who rushed to join the French as they progressed through Mayo were not patriots at heart. Many came forward for the opportunity to loot, pillage and generally wreak havoc on their Protestant neighbours. Others signed up for the chance to get free clothing and footwear.

> *"The French army is said to have at their landing at Killala Bay amounted to 1,060 men, who by various accidents have been reduced to 800. The General, Humbert, had distributed amongst the Rebels, arms and cloathing for 3000 men, but has never been able to collect more than 1500 of them for service. In short, they find themselves baffled, disappointed and betrayed, insomuch that they have begun to quarrel among themselves; some veteran Grenadiers, from the army of Italy, have remonstrated very loudly with their General, as*

having inveigled them to utter destruction. Upon the whole, we are happy that the experiment has been made; those of the invading army who may chance to return home will, no doubt, most feelingly demonstrate to their Rulers the wild absurdity of hoping to succeed in an invasion of Ireland."

Hampshire Chronicle - Monday 19 November 1798

This is a translation of Humbert's first report to the Directory. It was brought to France by Admiral Savary before he departed Kilcummin.

"Extract of a letter from General Humbert, written to the Minister of the Marine.
"Head-quarters, Killala, Ireland.
6th, Fructidor, (23rd. Aug.) At last, in spite of the English, we are on shore, and masters of Killala. Everything promises us the most complete success. I cannot sufficiently recommend the gallant seamen, who have conducted us to this coast. Citizen Savary, Chief of the Division, and the three Captains charged with the expedition, do infinite credit to your choice.
(Signed) "HUMBERT."

Chester Chronicle - Friday 28 September

Here, Humbert had to admit defeat. This dispatch was sent to the Directory after he was taken prisoner.

> *"Lichfield, Vendemiaire, September 23"*
> *"Citizens Directors, after having obtained the greatest successes, & made the arms of the French Republic to triumph during my stay in Ireland, I have at length been obliged to submit to a superior force of 30,000 troops commanded by Lord Cornwallis. I am a prisoner of war upon my parole."*
> HUMBERT"
>
> Chester Chronicle - Friday 28 September 1798

At this stage of proceedings, Humbert had left Castlebar as the enemy forces were closing in on his position.

> *"DUBLIN CASTLE, Sept. 2, 1798.*
> *Advices were this day received from the Lord Lieutenant's head-quarters, at Knock-hill, dated the 1st. Inst. His Excellency was advancing towards the enemy, and Col. Crawford is pushing his patroles to Castlebar. It appears that the numbers of the enemy have been exaggerated, and that they have been joined by a very inconsiderable number of the inhabitants."*
> *Tuesday, September 04, (Dublin Evening Post) 1798*

"SATURDAY, SEPTEMBER 29.
Yesterday fifty-one Frenchmen, made prisoners at Killala and Ballina were brought to town and conveyed to the Pigeon-house. These men seem to have been left behind the main body in the above places for the purpose of organizing and bringing, if possible, such of the natives as may join the invaders, to some degree of order and subordination, but by what has appeared, those wretches who did join them, having nothing in view save plunder and bloodshed, completely baffled every effort exerted for the purpose. The officers taken on the above occasion were yesterday lodged at Corbett's hotel, Capel-st.
A considerable number of the rebels who had been spared at Killala on suing for mercy and delivering up their arms, were on Thursday guarded down to the water side in order to their being transported from this country."

October 03, (Finns Leinster Journal)

"Letters received yesterday from Sligo, mention that the French fleet which appeared off Killala had entirely disappeared. Some of the persons that simply went on board them from the shore, imagining them to be British ships,

from their having hoisted English colours, have been carried off to sea."

November 01, (Freemans Journal)

It seems that Savary's ships made a second and very much unrecorded return trip to Killala Bay with additional troops and supplies to reinforce Humbert. There is little mention of this re-appearance of the three frigates that first appeared in Killala Bay. From other newspaper sources, those ships appeared again but were unable to land either men or materials because of the presence of Royal Navy ships on the lookout for further French attempts to foster rebellion. However, this and other newspaper accounts were depending on unreliable sources. There is no record of French frigates being captured off the north Mayo coast at this time.

"We have the pleasure to learn, that by letters received in town yesterday, intelligence is received, that two of the French frigates of the last squadron, which appeared off Killala, have been captured and brought in there by some of his Majesty's ships of war."

Tuesday, November 13, (Freemans Journal)

The numbers mentioned here, 15,000 rebels from Mayo being on the run in the mountains of Connemara, would appear to be somewhat exaggerated, to put it mildly!

"THURSDAY, OCTOBER 3.

A letter received yesterday from the county Mayo mentions, that the two rebel leaders named Jordan and Gannon, who had for some time past with a number of their followers, lurked in the mountains of Connemara, and for the apprehension of whom a considerable reward had been offered, have surrendered to Gen. Trench, throwing themselves on the mercy of the Government:- Their wretched followers, amounting to upwards of 15,000, will of course be obliged to act in a similar manner and insurgency in that quarter be completely annihilated."

Saturday, October 05, (Finns Leinster Journal)

The treatment of the rebels was in stark contrast to the prisoner of war status the French enjoyed.

"SLIGO, Sept. 21.
We are sorry to state that the rebels have been for these four weeks past in the full and undisturbed possession of Killala, Ballina, and the barony of Tyrawley. What then must be the situation, anxiety and distress of the loyal inhabitants of that extensive reach of country, many of whom have been driven from their homes, and depending for support of themselves and families on the bounty of friends

and relatives, while others without a possibility of receiving succour or relief, are suffering we know not to what extent of calamity, prisoners in the hands of ruthless villains. Is it possible that Government know nothing of this? Surely it cannot be; or otherwise in such great length of time some great and effective measures would be taken to put an end to the troubles of this hitherto peaceful country, and to restore the industrious and loyal to their homes, their properties and their families. This is a delicate subject and we forbear to push it further.

By a letter from a gentleman in Castlebar we learn that the rebels are in great force in the mountains of Westport.

By order of Lord Portarlington, who commands the garrison, a Court Martial on Monday last to try such rebels as were brought in from the country and which still continues to sit.

Tuesday last, Thomas Carroll, fisherman was found guilty of joining the French and carrying arms at Killala, and Daniel Scanlan, a deserter from the Longford militia, was also found guilty of the like offence and were both, pursuant to their sentence, executed on a tree in the Green Fort, on the above day."

Saturday, September 29, (Finns Leinster Journal)

When Humbert departed from Castlebar, he directed the bulk of the men he had left behind in Killala to meet him enroute as he marched eastwards. Only a total of four officers were left behind to keep law and order and to safeguard the lives and property of the Protestant population.

This was always going to be an impossible task as the English forces had pulled out of every town and district in all of Mayo, bar the southern strip from Hollymount southwards. There were literally thousands of rebels and they were out of control.

Inevitably, there was widespread looting and destruction of property, but the amazing fact remains that no blood was spilt. At least, that is what Bishop Stock recorded in his memoirs.

However, while none lost their lives in this savage period of destruction and pillage, the loyalist population and many of the more prosperous Catholics suffered substantial loss of animals and property.

> *"Extract of a letter from Addergoold, dated Sept. 22.*
> *"The whole of this country is entirely laid waste, and all the Protestants have been obliged to leave their houses, which are every day a-burning, from about ten miles from this to Westport and Newport: not one beast has been left to the Protestant inhabitants for the space of 50 miles to the westward and along the sea coast to the farthest part of Iris."*

This was written when the English forces were closing in on Killala and the insurgents knew there was no escape for them.

> *"Extract of a Letter from Castlebar, Sept. 24.*
> *I have pleasing news to communicate to you that*
> *General Trench marched from hence the 22 inst. for*
> *Ballina, whose force and those who marched in*
> *other directions, gave a total defeat to the Rebels*
> *at Killala, where numbers of them were*
> *slaughtered. Few prisoners were taken, among*
> *them some of their chiefs. The insurgents*
> *were completely surrounded. The Earl*
> *of Portarlington with his army marched against*
> *them from Sligo; the Armagh militia from Foxford;*
> *General Trench to the mountain road and a body of*
> *the Fraser regiment were stationed behind the*
> *mountain to prevent a retreat of the Rebels to Erris.*
> *Finding themselves hemmed in they fought*
> *desperately for a short while but with little effect.*
> *In this engagement, one of the military was killed*
> *and one wounded of the Kerry Militia. A small rebel*
> *party is at Knockmore, they threaten to attack this*
> *town tonight, but if they do, they will meet with a*
> *severe reception. All the prisoners who were in the*
> *hands of the desperadoes at Killala, have been*
> *released, among them the Bishop; he and others*
> *would have been put to death by the Rebels, were it*
> *not for the interference of a French officer. In their*
> *outrages last week, they showed great desperation,*

and their leaders gave directions "that the life of no Protestant, from the cradle to the crutch, should be spared." Freemans Journal Thursday, September 27, 1798

About the Author

Eamonn Henry is a retired schoolteacher, a native of Swinford, County Mayo and lives in Dublin.

He is the author of "The Little Book of Mayo" and "Historic Tales of Mayo," both commissioned by The History Press, Ireland and is the webmaster of www.mayogodhelpus.com, the popular Mayo-related website.

Printed in Great Britain
by Amazon